Running a Meeting That Works

Third Edition

Robert F. Miller and Marilyn Pincus

BARRON'S

All inquiries should be addressed to:
Barron's Educational Series, Inc.
250 Wireless Boulevard
Hauppauge, New York 11788
http://www.barronseduc.com

Library of Congress Catalog Card No. 2003058260

International Standard Book No. 0-7641-2450-1

Library of Congress Cataloging-in-Publication Data
Miller, Robert F. (Robert Finch), 1944–
    Running a meeting that works / Robert F. Miller and
Marilyn Pincus. — 3rd ed.
        p.   cm. — (Barron's business success guide)
    ISBN 0-7641-2450-1
    1. Business meetings.   I. Pincus, Marilyn.   II. Title.
III. Business success guide.

    HF5734.5.M56   2004
    658.4'56—dc22   2003058260
                                                              CIP

PRINTED IN CHINA
9 8 7 6 5 4 3 2 1

Contents

◆

Introduction

One of the most famous—or perhaps infamous—meetings in all of English literature concludes with the stuffing of one participant into a teapot.

Probably that has not happened in your experience, however often you've felt the urge. But it's not really stretching the point to compare the typical business meeting with the Mad Hatter's tea party in *Alice's Adventures in Wonderland,* in which the seating arrangements are chaotic, the Mad Hatter speaks nonsense, the March Hare is rude, and the Dormouse sleeps through the proceedings. Nobody takes charge, the conversation goes in circles, and nothing is accomplished. Sound familiar?

Meetings can be one of the most productive tools of the work environment for stimulating ideas, fostering a sense of team spirit, generating plans of action, providing valuable guidance, and consequently improving productivity. All too often, however, they are a complete waste of valuable time and energy. At one time *Industry Week* magazine estimated that $37 billion is wasted every year on poorly planned or poorly led meetings.

This book provides you with a commonsense approach to running a meeting that works. It offers a step-by-step process, starting with the decision to hold a meeting and ending with the final report on the proceedings. There are chapters on preparations for the meeting, taking charge, encouraging participation, handling difficult situations, using collateral materials and audiovisuals, and concluding and assessing a meeting.

This is a book about communication, about how people can come together with a shared purpose and accomplish their goals by talking with one another. It is about knowing what you want, organizing your thoughts, and articulating your ideas. It is about listening to and respecting the feelings and opinions of others. There are no clever gimmicks or mathematical formulas for success; running a meeting that works is as simple (which is not to say easy) as applying natural human communication skills to the work environment in a productive way.

What constitutes a meeting? There are conventions in faraway places, weekly staff meetings, and presentations aimed at landing a new account. There are creative sessions, bargaining sessions, and training sessions. There are sales and marketing meetings, press conferences, political meetings, and the annual meeting of the Order of the Garter. There are staff meetings and informational, problem-solving, and decision-making meetings. There are gatherings of three and assemblies of thousands.

It would be nice if this book were able to provide guidance in running all kinds of meetings, but its aim is less broad. This is a book about running the typical business meeting, the kind that takes place regularly in every office in America and that requires a leader to guide a small group of people through a communication process in a limited amount of time.

Whose idea is it to hold the meeting? The answer to that question has a major effect on the answers to many other questions raised in the following pages. Have you been asked to lead a meeting, or did you decide to hold it yourself? Whether it's deciding whom you should invite to participate, what the agenda should be, or what the meeting's goal is, much depends on who is calling the shots. Just how the advice in the next few chapters applies to your specific situation depends on which decisions you are able to make. Bear this in mind as you read the book. We don't live in a perfect world, alas, and it may be impossible to keep the Mad Hatter away from your next meeting. This book will, however, provide some useful guidance no matter how your role as meeting leader has been defined or limited. At the very least, it will help you keep the Dormouse out of the teapot.

Chapter 1

A Blueprint for Success:

Know Your Purpose

"*Would you tell me, please, which way
 I ought to go from here?*"
"*That depends a good deal on where you
 want to get to,*" *said the Cat.*

—*Alice's Adventures in Wonderland*

"What are we doing here?"

How many times have you asked yourself that question while sitting through a meeting that seems to have no direction? You glance at your watch, draw caricatures of the boss, and imagine your desk piling higher and higher with work that you must get done before the end of the day.

Studies of corporate work patterns indicate that some business executives spend as much as half their work lives in meetings of one kind or another. But how often are these meetings worth the preparation, time, and thought they demand of participants, as well as leaders? Isn't it true that most meeting participants, even those who really want to accomplish something, are convinced that the meeting will be disappointing? Why are most meetings so frustrating? The culprit, invariably, is a meeting leader without a sense of direction.

KNOW YOUR PURPOSE FOR MEETING

> *The first and most important step in running a meeting that works is knowing your purpose for calling the meeting.*

The way you formulate your purpose in calling the meeting is critical to helping you organize your thoughts. Consider these examples.

"I've gathered you here today because we haven't had a meeting in a while." WRONG.

"I've gathered you here because I need to know what each of you is working on." RIGHT.

"The purpose of this meeting is to discuss the new product launch scheduled for tomorrow." WRONG.

"The purpose of this meeting is for me to tell you a few things about the product launch scheduled for tomorrow." RIGHT.

"We're here today because we've got to come up with some ideas for restructuring this department." WRONG.

"We're here today because I have some ideas about restructuring this department and I need your opinions on the subject." RIGHT.

A wise professor once said, "If you can't express your thoughts so that others can understand them, you don't know what your thoughts are." Know exactly what you hope to accomplish in the meeting and make that purpose clear from the outset.

It is not enough to want to discuss a subject; the discussion must have a focus. Do you want to discuss the subject of raises for everyone in the department because it's an interesting topic, or because you want to reach a decision about whether to raise salaries?

In formulating the purpose of the meeting it is often helpful to ask the question "Why?" Suppose the boss comes to you and says, "We need to have a meeting to talk about a new marketing plan." Ask why. What does he or she want to accomplish? Another example: Imagine you're put in charge of a project involving four other people. You think to yourself, "I'd better call a meeting." First, ask yourself why. What, specifically, do you want to accomplish?

DECIDING THE PURPOSE OF THE MEETING
The *purpose* of the meeting is not the same as the *subject* of the meeting. Suppose you call your staff together to plan the marketing strategy of a new product. The subject of the meeting is the new product;

> *the purpose of the meeting—what you hope to accomplish—is the exchange of ideas and information necessary to create a marketing plan.*

In determining your purpose, it is often helpful to reduce it to its simplest terms. On the most basic level, there are only two purposes for any meeting—*to give information* or *to get information.* (Meetings may, of course, involve a combination of the two.)

Your first step in determining your purpose is to ask yourself, "Do I want to give information, get information, or both?" Your second step is to ask yourself, "What information do I want to give, get, or exchange?" For example, do you want a report from each attendee on his or her activities during the last week? Do you want to provide your staff with the schedule of events for tomorrow's product launch? Do you want input on your ideas for restructuring the department?

> *If you know exactly what you want to accomplish going into a meeting, chances are you'll have it coming out.*

As you plan the meeting, bear in mind two words of caution: Be realistic. Can you accomplish your purpose? Do you have and understand the information you need to provide to others? Do they have the information you need? Do you have the time you need? Will the people you need to accomplish your purpose be at the meeting? Do you have the control or the decision-making power you need to accomplish your goal? Are you prepared for the meeting?

Many of these questions will be addressed in later chapters; all must be weighed as you decide on a realistic purpose for the meeting.

A meeting that works is a wondrous, exciting event. Sparks fly, gears shift, lightbulbs flash on, and ideas bounce into receptive minds. Some meetings take a minute, others an hour or two; but it is always time well spent when the purpose of the meeting is understood, articulated, and accomplished.

Chapter 2

Why Have a Meeting?:

Is This the Best Way to Accomplish the Purpose?

. . . it would have made a dreadfully ugly child: but it makes rather a handsome pig, I think.

—Alice's Adventures in Wonderland

Business communications come in many forms—memos, telephone calls, webcasts, online chats, reports, faxes. Meetings are only one of many options. So before going any further, it might be wise to decide if having a meeting is the best way to accomplish your purpose.

WHY HAVE A MEETING?

The decision whether to have a meeting depends on a number of factors, such as the need you are attempting to satisfy. There are many possibilities:

◆ a need to pass along information or collect it from other people

◆ a need to resolve an office conflict or a difference of opinion

◆ a need for a majority decision or evaluation on some issue

◆ a need to generate a sense of team spirit

◆ a need to be sure that the staff understands the nature of the next project

◆ a need to provide training in the use of new equipment

◆ a need to change a few people's minds on an issue

◆ a need for an immediate response to a problem

◆ a need to persuade a client to use your services

Some of these needs can be best met in a meeting; others cannot. Most can be met in a number of ways, depending on your specific circumstances, talents, and work situation. Information, for example, can be provided in a meeting, memo, or report, depending on the nature of the information. An office conflict is probably best resolved by bringing the interested parties face to face privately. A majority decision can be obtained by a show of hands in a meeting, by correspondence, or telephone, depending on whether voters have advance access to the material being voted upon. Training can be accomplished via a manual or a meeting; much depends on the nature of the subject. A meeting may change some opinions, but so might one-to-one conversations. And a well-conceived, visually impressive written proposal may be just as effective in winning a client as a verbal presentation. For generating team spirit, however, a meeting can be one of the most effective tools.

To determine whether a meeting is the best tool for you to use, consider the following:

COST

At first glance, the cost of gathering a few people in the conference room may not seem like a big deal. A few simple calculations, however, reveal a different story. First of all, there are the salaries of the participants: The difference between the cost of an hour or two of your time alone and the cost of that time multiplied by the number of participants at their value per hour to the company can be significant. Then there is the cost to the company of your preparing for the meeting and the cost of any assistants helping you, as well as the cost of the time spent by other participants as they prepare for the meeting.

Take a meeting of ten people whose values per hour to the company are as follows: two supervisors at $100 per hour, three managers at $50 per hour, three account executives at $30 per hour, and two assistants at $15 per hour. A two-hour meeting of this group, not counting preparation time, costs the company $940.

Then there are the more tangible costs: materials, room rentals, refreshments, secretarial services, and possibly transportation. A recent "Meetings Market Report" by *Meetings & Conventions* magazine reveals that meeting planners spend 79 percent of their budgets on accommodations, transportation, and food and beverages. Your meeting may not require all these components. Still, considering that a meeting planner's budget does not include cost to the company of participants' time, whatever costs you do incur may be significant.

Any kind of a meeting is expensive. In making your decision to hold a meeting, always compare its cost with the cost of alternatives. The only time cost does not matter is when there is no alternative to the meeting.

RESTRICTIONS

There is no point in scheduling a meeting if unavoidable restrictions make its success unlikely. Ask yourself the following questions:

◆ Do I have time to prepare for the meeting?

◆ Do other participants have the time to prepare themselves?

◆ Are all the necessary participants available and willing to attend?

If you cannot answer yes to all three questions, a meeting will be a waste of time.

The very nature of a meeting imposes certain restrictions on its effectiveness. Meetings are run and attended by human beings; put two or more humans in the same room and the chances for disagreement, confusion, and inefficiency are great. After all, each of us is full of opinion, ideas, and emotions. Not every need is best met in a meeting. If you

◆ have a simple message to deliver

◆ need a simple answer to a question

◆ have information to give that requires no immediate response

◆ don't have time to consider every side of the question or debate each issue

◆ are more persuasive or forceful on paper than in person

>*there may be more effective ways of accomplishing your purpose than having a meeting.*

WHEN TO HAVE A MEETING

So how do you decide if a meeting is the best tool to use?

Assuming that the cost is not prohibitive, that there is time to prepare adequately, and that all the necessary players are available, a meeting is the right choice if

1. **the interaction of opinions is necessary to create an idea, plan, or project.** Meetings are the way to go if a creative session in which the exchange of half-formed ideas leading to the generation of a fully formed concept is essential.

2. **group dynamics are essential to the accomplishment of the purpose.** Meetings are valuable tools for generating team spirit at a sales meeting or staff meeting as you work toward a dynamic team presentation aimed at winning a new client.

3. **time restrictions limit other options.** Meetings may be necessary in a situation in which group consensus is required but there is no time to circulate reports and wait for responses.

4. **the subject is sufficiently complex as to require interaction and explanation.** Meetings may be the best way to introduce a new product line or to train staff to use a sophisticated piece of equipment.

5. **the boss says to hold a meeting.** Enough said.

A BAD (BUT OFTEN TEMPTING) REASON TO HOLD A MEETING

The boss hands you a new assignment. "Double the company's profits—by tomorrow," you are instructed. You begin to organize your strategy. There are memos to write, assignments to make, information to gather and distribute. Overwhelmed, you say to yourself, "Maybe it would be easiest to have a meeting." Don't. All too often, a meeting seems to be the simple solution to a seemingly difficult situation. It *may be* the right solution, but don't hold a meeting simply because the alternatives seem daunting.

You may hate to write reports or memos. You may feel lost without colleagues with whom to try out new ideas. You may be afraid you can't handle an assignment alone. You might prefer not to do the research yourself. You may even want an excuse for having lunch at company expense or to escape the rest of your responsibilities. These are not reasons to have a meeting. Resist using meetings as an escape. Consider your options and put meetings to use where they are most effective.

Chapter 3

Preparing for the Meeting:

What, Who, When, Where, and for How Long

"Begin at the beginning," the King said, very gravely, *"and go on till you come to the end: then stop."*

—*Alice's Adventures in Wonderland*

When you've decided what you want to accomplish at your meeting, you have taken the most important step in preparing yourself to be the meeting leader. From here on, it is a matter of organization.

Journalists are taught a basic rule of news reporting: Tell who, what, when, and where in as few words as possible at the top of the story. In preparing to lead a meeting, you can apply the same rule by asking yourself these questions:

◆ What kind of meeting do I want?

◆ Whom should I invite?

◆ When should the meeting be scheduled?

◆ Where should I hold the meeting?

There's one other question you should answer: How long should the meeting last?

After you decide the purpose of your meeting and answer these questions, you'll be almost ready to take charge.

WHAT KIND OF MEETING DO I WANT?

There are two basic types of meetings: discussions and briefings. Discussion meetings are based on interaction: Participants share ideas and opinions, contribute information, and possibly make decisions through some kind of voting process. Staff meetings, creative meetings, and problem-solving meetings are examples of interactive discussion meetings.

Briefings are meetings in which one or more speakers provide information to a group of listeners. There may be little group interaction apart from a few questions from the audience. News conferences, sales presentations, and training sessions are examples of briefings.

Of course, many meetings are a combination of briefing and group discussion. Your first task is to decide which type of meeting best suits your need. If your primary purpose is to communicate information to the group, perhaps a briefing is the most efficient way to go. However, if you need information from several people or if there is a problem to solve or a plan to create, a discussion meeting is the likely choice.

WHOM DO I INVITE?

At a large public relations firm in New York, a certain kind of memo is circulated frequently. It says something like this: "We hope to pitch a new client, a theme amusement park in the Gobi Desert. There will be a creative meeting to discuss ways of promoting this product. Everyone is welcome; we need good ideas!" The memo is sent to dozens of executives, including those who promote everything from cameras and controversial drugs to candy bars and polyester clothing. The meeting date arrives; no one, other than the staff of the memo sender, shows up.

There is a simple but often difficult-to-follow rule for inviting people to a meeting:

Invite only those people who need to be there.

That means including only those individuals who have something specific to contribute, whether it is information or expertise. It may mean the people to whom you have information to give. A scatter-shot approach—"I guess I'll just throw this wide open and hope someone shows up with a valuable contribution"—is a waste of your time.

Invite only those people you are willing to listen to.

Have you ever tried to make a contribution in a meeting, only to find your ideas being dismissed or ignored by the leader? It happens all the time. This is not only rude to the individual concerned but unproductive, a waste of everyone's time. In determining your list of participants, invite only those people whose contributions you are willing to listen to and consider seriously.

"Why is Dracula in this meeting?" someone may ask. "You know, politics," is the invariable answer.

> Do *not use the protocol list to select meeting participants.*

Admittedly, this is the most difficult rule to follow because office politics are an unfortunate part of the work environment, and it's often difficult to avoid inviting someone for no other reason than that it's the political thing to do. Often, that person is The Boss.

But there's a good reason to try. Unless that person has another reason, such as expertise, for being in the meeting, a supervisor's presence can serve to distract participants from the subject under discussion and complicate the task of the leader, who now has to run a meeting and "play politics" as well. In addition, from the perspective of the unneeded guest, the invitation may be considered an irritating obligation. Invitation by protocol can be a no-win situation for all concerned; the best advice is to try your best to avoid it.

HOW MANY PEOPLE SHOULD I INVITE TO THE MEETING?

The answer to this question depends on two factors: what kind of meeting it is and how many people *need* to be there. A study by the Center for Advanced Studies in Behavioral Sciences in Palo Alto, California, found that the larger the group, the longer it took to make decisions; further, the study found that the decisions were identical to those made by smaller groups discussing the same topic.

If you are planning a group discussion, the general rule is, the fewer participants, the better. Certainly there should be no more than a dozen. And it's often wise to take a page from Oriental philosophy and stick to odd numbers—three, five, seven, nine—particularly if decisions are to be made. An even number of participants tends to encourage camps or sides that can immobilize a meeting's progress; an uneven number of participants is more difficult to divide up.

For briefings, the number of participants is limited only by the size of the room and the strength of your voice. Whatever the type of meeting you have planned, the most important rule is to invite only the people who need to be there.

A final note on the guest list: Invitations are just the first step. Participants also need to know what is expected of them in the meeting. This aspect of preparation is discussed in Chapter 5.

WHEN SHOULD I HAVE THE MEETING?

It has been said that you should always buy a car that came off the assembly line on Tuesday, Wednesday, or Thursday. Cars assembled on Monday are suspect because the workers are just back from a weekend and may be tired, distracted, or inattentive, and those that roll out on Friday may be victims of the T.G.I.F. syndrome. Similarly, teachers of small children try to do the "serious" stuff—English, social studies, math, science—in the morning, because by afternoon, attention spans are short. Perhaps meetings work by the same rules.

There are several simple guidelines to follow in deciding when to hold a meeting:

1. **Allow Enough Time for Preparation.** This means several things: time for you to invite participants and prepare your materials and presentation; time for participants to prepare what is expected of them; and time for support staff to prepare the handout materials for the meeting. Deadlines also must be considered; if the meeting's purpose is to prepare a report or presentation for a specific event, be sure you allow time to have the meeting and then do the necessary follow-up work before the deadline. Don't get caught finishing the work after the party's over.

In timing your meeting, work backward from the deadline— "The report is due at the end of the month. We need one week to prepare documents *after* the meeting. I'll have to review those documents. That will take three days, and the staff needs a week to prepare *for* the meeting, so I'd better schedule it for . . ."

2. **Schedule Meetings on a Date When All Necessary Players Are Available.** It makes sense to confirm attendance in advance of setting the final date.

3. **Avoid Scheduling a Meeting on Holidays, Long Weekends, and at the Beginning or End of the Week.** This may seem obvious, but a quick glance at the calendar is always a good idea.

4. **Morning Meetings Are More Productive than Those Scheduled Late in the Day.** Our attention spans may be slightly longer than those of children, but there is a tendency to become more and more enmeshed in work as the day proceeds. Late in the day, meeting participants may be distracted by other tasks and therefore less forthcoming in their contributions. They may also feel some resentment at having to drop what they are doing to attend a meeting.

5. **Don't Mix Business with Pleasure.** Attempts to combine a meeting with lunch, dinner, or a reception often meet with disappointment. Attention to the serious matters at hand is diluted, particularly at dinner or reception meetings. There's nothing wrong with socializing; just don't try to do business at the same time.

If you must schedule a meeting at a mealtime, try breakfast. Breakfast meetings tend to be well attended (because you catch people before their workday starts), short, and productive.

If you must have a meeting with lunch, dinner, or drinks, be sure to use adjoining rooms—one for the meeting, the other for socializing. The meeting *always* should come first. And avoid the pitfall of scheduling business between courses of a meal, unless you don't care that no one is listening. Such a schedule is *always* a mistake.

WHERE SHOULD I HOLD THE MEETING?

A press briefing took place recently in an elegant restaurant in New York at breakfast time, when the restaurant was closed to other patrons. The service was excellent, the food superb, and the setting magnificent. The invited guests were clustered in close proximity to the speaker, who rose to thank them all for coming out so early in the day. He went on to discuss his company's exciting new services. The only problem was the lovely waterfall that made the setting so magnificent—it completely drowned out his words.

The choice of location for a meeting depends on several factors, including the presence or absence of waterfalls. Of course, you may have little choice in the matter, but, assuming you can select a location, keep in mind the following considerations:

1. **Make the Location Convenient.** Be sure that the location is accessible to all participants—that is, within easy reach of their respective offices.

2. Pick a Neutral Spot. If the purpose of your meeting is to resolve conflicts or solve a problem, it may be best to pick a neutral corner—a location that gives no advantage to any group or individual.

3. Be Sensitive to Politics. Some meetings require a sensitivity to politics. If you're making a presentation to a prospective client, for example, it is wise to go to the client's office rather than ask the client to come to yours. If The Boss is an essential participant in your meeting and his office is on the thirty-fourth floor, it may be expedient to hold the meeting in his conference room rather than yours.

4. Check the Cost. Be sure the location of your choice can be accommodated in your meeting's budget.

5. Pick the Right Facilities. This consideration may be the most important of all. Does your location have the appropriate seating for your type of meeting? Does it offer the right level of comfort? (First class may be all right for airlines, but too plush a setting elsewhere may be distracting.) Do you have access to whatever audiovisual equipment you require? Are there catering facilities suitable to your needs? Is there access for people who use wheelchairs?

HOW LONG SHOULD THE MEETING LAST?

A meeting should last as long as it takes to accomplish its purpose. The secret, of course, is having a realistic purpose. There are no hard-and-fast rules about the length of meetings; some are over in minutes, whereas others drag on for hours. Certainly, no meeting session should last more than one hour without a break of ten minutes or more.

You should remember that you're dealing with people, not machines. Attention spans vary, and even the most interesting subjects in the world pall after being discussed for more than an hour or two at any one time. Can you honestly expect people to stay interested in marketing plans or staff reports for any longer? If your session lasts more than two hours, your purpose is too ambitious for one meeting. The meeting's productivity is likely to be less than cost-effective, and you should consider scheduling two or more sessions.

PREPARING FOR THE MEETING

Having asked *what, who, when, where,* and *how long,* you face only one more task in preparing for a meeting: doing the work you need to do to be well informed.

Good intentions on the part of a meeting leader mean little if he or she enters the meeting unprepared. You know the purpose of the meeting and what you want to accomplish. You've decided whom to invite, when and where to hold the meeting, and what to expect from the participants. Now you need to determine what you expect from yourself. As a final step in preparing yourself to lead the meeting with confidence, ask the following questions:

◆ What information do I need to lead this meeting?

◆ Is that information readily available? Where can I get it?

◆ Do I need to prepare any written materials?

◆ How long will it take me to prepare myself?

◆ Do I need assistance in preparing for the meeting?

Then do the work.

Note: At the end of this book is a checklist you can use as a guide in preparing yourself and others for a meeting.

Chapter 4

Preparing Yourself:

Begin with a Winning Image and Attitude

She was now only ten inches high, and her face brightened up at the thought that she was now the right size for going through the little door into that lovely garden.

—*Alice's Adventures in* Wonderland

The way you look affects the way you feel and the image you project to others. When others look at you and see someone who is radiant, self-assured, and enthusiastic, they fashion their responses to you with bias. They're prejudiced. They can't help themselves—it's an automatic response. As a result, you can manipulate your look and take advantage of this phenomenon to achieve goals.

DRESS FOR MEETING SUCCESS

Even when you're typically careful about planning your work wardrobe, pay special attention to your meeting wardrobe. Here's why:

◆ Colors can make you appear as a bold person or a muted person. A red or pink jacket, for example, earns a sit-up-and-take-notice reaction, whereas a gray or blue jacket tends to invite a same-old, same-old response. Of course, you can excite your coworkers with your brilliant, new ideas while wearing a blue jacket, but you prepare them for the excitement when you walk into the meeting room wearing boldly colored garments. Don't rush out to buy a red jacket if that's impractical, but do consider purchasing something in a new, spirited color, even just a scarf or tie. Remember, however, a jacket, suit, or dress covers more area so it delivers a hard-to-miss message. (If you always wear bold colors, perhaps choose muted tones to attract attention and promote interest.)

◆ If you look casual, your performance may be perceived as relaxed and frivolous. Loose-fitting garments that flutter can make it appear that your assertions will flutter, too.

◆ If you look formal, your performance may be perceived to be all business, serious. Crisp collars, tailored, form-fitting garments, and sharp creases support a no-nonsense position.

◆ Classic clothing symbolizes tradition, experience, and an attitude of general acceptance, whereas faddish clothing endorses a penchant for traveling in new, uncharted territory.

If you find these observations baffling, consider seeking the services of a professional image expert. He or she can assist you in selecting a business wardrobe that supports your personal goals. This will include "power" clothing you'll probably want to wear when you attend meetings.

Of course, you may decide to wear clothing that sends a false or confusing message. If you want to soften up the opposition, for example, you may decide to arrive at the conference table looking all "spit and polish" even when you know you'll compromise to resolve issues.

WHAT YOU SEE IS WHAT YOU GET

Body language is a window to your soul. If you've never thought about it before, think about it!

Stride into the meeting room with your head erect and your shoulders square and you send a different message than if you slink into the meeting room with your eyes cast downward and your posture best described as sag and drag.

You may expect the boss to be ready to read the riot act to you. If you arrive looking like a frightened rabbit, the boss may proceed as expected. If, however, you arrive looking composed and dignified, and you maintain that appearance, the boss may feel less and less inclined to assail you. Your suave and confident manner could be quite disarming. After all, the boss is affected by body language, too.

Body language is potent stuff! When you're preparing for a meeting, it serves you well to consider what your movements say to others.

P – Posture—upright, not sagging. Capable.
O – Obviously caring. Smiling, listening. Involved.
W – Walk tall. No dragging or slouching. Secure.
E – Eye contact, direct. Intent.
R – Relaxed body, especially arms, hands, shoulders. Calm.

You can send a message that you're capable, involved, secure, intent, and calm without saying a word.

YOUR A.Q. (ASSERTIVENESS QUOTIENT)

Weigh your assertiveness tendencies. If the scale tips too far in either direction, ask yourself whether or not it's in your best interest to act aggressively or passively. It takes only moments to reflect on your A.Q. The assessment, however, can prevent should-have, would-have, or could-have regrets from arising.

If you're someone's mentor, a meeting environment is an excellent proving ground for your prodigy. If he or she tends to be passive, you may want to take the individual under your wing before the meeting and discuss the key words and phrases he or she can use to demonstrate conviction and a willingness to get involved. (Note: Some assertiveness experts recommend using "I" language, meaning sentences that begin with the word *I*: I see, I feel, I believe, I noticed.) These preparations can embolden new or inexperienced individuals to test the waters.

If your prodigy is a trifle too zealous, it's a good time to discuss goals and boundaries. This newcomer may have to be reminded that patience is a virtue. A few words of advice delivered just before a meeting are likely to be remembered and acted upon.

Just before the meeting is a good time to mentally prepare yourself, too. Use any favorite personal techniques to banish distraction and preoccupation from your thoughts so you walk into the room with a clean slate. You'll be free to concentrate on matters at hand, and your listening skills will automatically be more finely tuned. For some folks, a few quiet moments just before taking on a new task works wonders.

PLEASE, BE SEATED

Will you sit in the front of the meeting room? Who will be seated nearby? Where you place yourself in the room sends a subtle message to others. Consider the following positions:

◆ Front and center—you're where the action is

◆ At the rear—you're a listener rather than a participant

◆ Anywhere else—you're in a neutral position

Whether you attend a church service, classroom lecture, office meeting, or any gathering where seats are unassigned, this pattern of positioning generally prevails. Pay attention the next time you're in any of these environments. Your chair can be more than a piece of furniture. It can be a declaration of your intended role at the meeting.

If a colleague promises to support the budget proposal you'll present but she sits at the rear of the room, she may only have told you what she thought you wanted to hear. If she's planning to rise to support you, she'll probably sit up front.

Does this seating strategy work 100 percent of the time? Absolutely not. Become a keen observer, however, and you'll be able to predict things to come without benefit of a crystal ball. Factor the telltale signals into your plans and you'll get your way more often than not.

WHICH WIZARD WEARS WHICH WRISTWATCH?

Practice opening lines so you don't get tongue-tied or veer off track. It's a practical, simple plan to follow. When you know you'll rise to support or refute some agenda item, remarks that are clear and crisp suggest to listeners that your words are well thought out. Once listeners adopt this belief, your remarks carry weight.

The Greek philosopher Aristotle referred to credibility as one of three indispensable pillars of persuasion. (The other two are fact and emotion.) A speaker who trips over words, utters too many ahs or ums, or in other ways neglects to make first comments count, risks establishing credibility.

Practicing your opening lines is one more way you can prepare yourself to look good at a meeting.

STAGING TECHNIQUES

Did you ever notice how props on a stage help to tell a story? Flowery wallpaper, a bowl of fruit on the table, and a basket of knitting yarn next to a frilly sofa where a cat lies napping set the stage for a homey encounter. These props constitute details, and details help support expectations.

Here are some props anyone might bring to a meeting:

◆ a gavel (large or small)

◆ an obviously expensive pen

◆ a well-worn briefcase, bursting at the seams

◆ reading glasses

◆ a writing pad tucked inside a personalized leather binder

Whether your props are personal things or standard business items, they help to set your stage.

You may not appear to be orderly or efficient when you carry a well-worn briefcase that's so stuffed with papers that you can't locate what you want quickly. Consider buying a new briefcase and get organized.

Reading glasses perched on the end of your nose may make you appear comical. You may want to check with your eye-care specialist for a suitable replacement.

LOOK FURTHER
If you'll be speaking at a lectern but the lectern shows serious signs of wear and tear, plan to step in front of the lectern when you speak, or arrange to have it draped with an attractive cloth cover.

If the room lighting is too bright or too dim, adjust the window coverings or ask facility maintenance people to make changes. Monitor extremes in air temperature, too. Listeners sitting in a dimly lit, warm room may take a nap. If there's one thing that can distract you from turning in a top performance, it's colleagues who are nodding off as you speak.

BACK TO BASICS

People function best when they're not too hungry or tired. Get sufficient sleep, take time to eat breakfast before you arrive at an early morning meeting, and attend to other basic needs so you don't find yourself feeling trapped in the conference room.

Recognize that as meeting leader, you're basically a salesperson. You're either attending the meeting to sell something (e.g., your ideas) or to discover what the competition has to offer, or maybe both.

If you're selling, be prepared to

◆ give them what they want.

◆ give them something more—a bonus—something unexpected, unnecessary, but wonderful.

If you're listening to a sales pitch, remember, these people are probably your internal customers:

◆ Listen carefully.

◆ Be prepared to satisfy your customers.

Exercise all the skills that separate successful salespeople from the wildly successful salespeople! This mind-set should put you into high gear.

Now, let the meeting begin.

AN EXIT POLL

People often talk about first impressions, but last impressions are arguably more valuable. At the conclusion of the meeting, document your last impressions. You can use the simple form that follows as a model. Refer to your exit poll responses the next time you attend a meeting with the same people or attend a meeting that has a similar agenda. Now, you'll benefit from what you already know but may otherwise forget.

MEETING TOPIC _____ Date _____

WHO ATTENDED? _____

MY FUNCTION _____

GENERAL ACHIEVEMENTS _____

HOW DID I DO? _____

CAN I DO BETTER? HOW? _____

This is a for-your-eyes-only document. Maintain it in a confidential file. If you're candid, this won't be an exercise in futility.

For example, when you answered How did I do? you may have written: "I got run over by BB. He had all last year's figures and current April figures on hand. I had only this quarter's numbers and didn't have April figures. The decision to dismiss two excellent staffers was made and I think it's a big mistake."

Based on that response, you may decide to collect more extensive data before you attend another meeting that relates to budget and staffing.

Chapter 5

Preparing Others:

Letting Participants Know Your Expectations

"The time has come," the Walrus said, "to talk of many things."

—*Alice's Adventures in Wonderland*

The phone rings. It's the boss's assistant, who says, "A meeting has been scheduled to develop next year's marketing plan." "Fine," you respond. "When is it?" "In five minutes," she says. Incredible but true; it happens all the time.

No matter how carefully you prepare to lead a meeting, your efforts will be for naught if you fail to prepare the other participants adequately as well. It's to your advantage to have well-prepared participants. Giving them enough time to do the research, prepare the report, check the files, or give some thought to the subject of the meeting is just one part of helping them to be ready.

PROVIDING THE NECESSARY INFORMATION

Essential to preparing the participants of a meeting is providing them with the information they need to make a valuable contribution.

1. **Tell Them the Purpose of the Meeting as well as the Subject.** "We are meeting to formulate a marketing plan for the Imperial Widget Company." Or, "There will be a staff meeting to outline the status of all current projects."

2. **Be Sure to Provide a Meeting Agenda.** There should be no surprises; a subject introduced without warning will be the subject of a fruitless discussion. All participants deserve the courtesy of knowing in advance all the topics to be raised in the meeting.

   The agenda is your road map. Don't leave it in a file or under a stack of papers when the meeting begins. Use it. It will help everyone navigate from start to finish without getting lost.

   Your agenda should be

   ◆ clear

   ◆ specific

   ◆ brief but not too brief

   Examples of agenda items:

(Good) ◆ Review the merits of two digital cameras.

(Better) ◆ Compare Nikon Coolpix 5000 with Canon Power Shot S50.

(Good) ◆ Allocate scholarship funds.

(Better) ◆ Available scholarship funds total $1,450. Applicants total five. Determine how much to award each recipient.

When you get into the habit of telling it like it is, you'll benefit, too. It will be easier for you to gauge the time required to dispense with each agenda item.

Allocate a time guesstimate to each topic. If you're overtime, shorten the agenda. If you have trouble guesstimating how much time to allow each agenda item, use a worst case scenario calculation. People won't mind if the meeting winds up early. Not only will you build credibility, but you'll be running a meeting that works! People can focus on matters at hand instead of keeping an eye on the clock.

3. Tell Them What Is Expected of Them. "Please be prepared to offer several ideas about how we might market Imperial Widgets." Or, "Please be prepared to report on the status of your projects." In some cases you can prepare a blanket directive to all participants; in other cases, you may need to make requests to individual attendees. Be specific in requesting the information you need.

4. Tell Them When and Where the Meeting Will Be Held and How Long You Expect It to Last.

There are three things you should remember when providing the information meeting participants need to prepare themselves:

1. **Allow Plenty of Time for Preparation.** Take into consideration what you expect of those invited to the meeting; give them time to prepare the report or to review their work. Above all, give them time to think about the purpose of the meeting and its subject.

> *The more you expect from meeting participants, the more time they should have to prepare.*

2. **Put It All in Writing.** Do not give instructions or describe expectations over the telephone, because you can never be sure that you have the full attention of the listener. At the moment of your call he or she might be deep in thought about something else, on another call, or spilling coffee. E-mail messages and facsimile transmissions can expedite communications. As you'll see below, these communication channels are subject to confirmation of receipt measures, too. Assume nothing. Verify.

3. **Confirm that All Participants Have Received the Message.** You or your assistant should confirm by telephone that your outline containing the purpose, agenda, and particulars of the meeting has been received and understood: "Hi, George. Did you get my memo about the meeting? Can you make it? Do you understand what I need from you? Great, see you next Thursday at 10 A.M."

> *A well-prepared participant is a productive participant. Do everything you can to make it possible for attendees to contribute productively to the meeting.*

Chapter 6

Who's in Charge Here?:

Do's and Don'ts for Guiding the Meeting

The players all played at once, without
waiting for turns, quarrelling all the while . . .
and in a very short time the Queen was in a
furious passion, and went stamping about,
and shouting, "Off with his head!"

—*Alice's Adventures in* Wonderland

This staff meeting actually took place:

Summoned for a 10 A.M. meeting, the staff assembled in a conference room and waited for The Boss. As minutes ticked by, various individuals drifted in and out of the room, fixed coffee, and chatted in the corners. At 10:15 The Boss arrived with a load of papers and, without a "Hello" or "Sorry I'm late," said, "We've got a lot of work to do."

Calling on one staff member for a progress report, The Boss began rustling through papers and searching through folders. Minutes later he left the room without warning, leaving the speaker in mid-sentence. A few minutes later, The Boss was back. "Go on," he said; as the speaker tried to pick up where she had left off, The Boss turned to his assistant and began a whispered conversation. Then he was across the room talking on the telephone, then back to his papers, then gone once more without warning. At no time did The Boss, the leader of the meeting, sit still, look a participant in the eye, and listen to a conversation. After more than an hour of reports and attempted discussions—all of which were constantly interrupted, broken off, or ignored—the leader concluded the meeting by saying, "I'm just not getting enough work out of you; I have to do everything myself."

This is a case of a meeting without a leader, despite the presence of someone ostensibly making the rules. Needless to say, the only accomplishments were exasperation and bruised feelings on the part of the staff and frustration on the part of The Boss. An extreme case, perhaps, but typical of how far too many meetings are run in offices throughout America, according to interviews with executives and meeting participants in offices across the country.

Running a meeting that works is really not very difficult. Essentially it requires two things of the leader:

> *Maintaining control over the proceedings and giving the meeting his or her undivided attention.*

Tim Hindle, author of *Managing Meetings (Essential Managers)*, Dorling-Kindersley First American Edition, April 1999, writes, "Control the meeting properly and you can keep the subject matter moving while at the same time allowing for open conversation between participants." Here are some suggestions that make taking charge easier:

Do Your Homework.

Come to the meeting prepared, having done the research, prepared the reports, or reviewed whatever material is to be discussed. Know the purpose of the meeting.

Remember the Process.

Every meeting has four steps: *presenting the information, evaluating the information, coming to a decision, and taking action.* An understanding of these steps should underlie everything you do to lead a meeting. The substance of each step, of course, varies, depending on your goal for the meeting; nevertheless, the four steps can be applied to virtually every kind of meeting.

Step 1, presenting the information, includes presenting the purpose of the meeting and the facts or ideas necessary to achieve the purpose: "Today we need to develop a plan to expand our sales force. I'd like each of you to offer some ideas on how to do that."

Step 2, evaluating the information, is the discussion phase in which all participants debate the merits of the ideas or facts already presented.

Step 3, coming to a decision, is the process of resolving the problem: "We are agreed, then, that the best way to expand the sales force would be to . . . Is that correct?"

Step 4, taking action, is the implementation of the decision. This stage begins with making assignments in the meeting and ends with following up on the actions decided on. In our example, this might mean asking one group of people to draft a final report on the sales force expansion, asking another person to discuss the matter with the personnel department, and asking yet another to meet with the accounting department. A timetable for completion of these tasks should be agreed upon before you adjourn the meeting. Then it's up to you to follow up in the weeks to come.

Distribute an Agenda.

What's agenda insurance? It's having a copy of the agenda waiting for each person who sits down at the meeting table. Of course, you distributed the agenda early on when you first announced the upcoming meeting. Still, this document is important and you underscore its importance by having a copy available to anyone who needs it when the meeting starts.

This technique silently announces: "Here's our road map, people. We're going to use it to help us navigate from start to finish without getting lost."

At future meetings with the same people, participants will be less likely to arrive at the meeting table without this document. After all, this agenda is your plan. Once you draft the plan, you expect to work your plan. Anything less is a waste of time.

AGENDA PREMIUMS
If the agenda format is consistent from meeting to meeting it will

◆ save time,

◆ serve as your checklist,

◆ be readily identified by recipients,

◆ subtly announce, "Here's something of value."

Why reinvent the wheel each time you write an agenda? Simply maintain a master document on your computer. As you scan the master, you'll be prompted to include all necessary components on the agenda you're about to generate.

Use a consistent

◆ color

◆ shape

◆ size

and you'll visually set the agenda apart from other material deposited on a person's desk.

Send agendas you generate via e-mail with a "look" that sets them apart, too. When margins are wider than usual or you choose Arial Slim instead of your usual Times New Roman font, agendas will be immediately recognizable.

If you run meetings by the book (preferably this book), the agenda will be well received. Coworkers will know they can rely on it to accurately report what to expect. They can prepare accordingly and won't waste their time.

When people arrive at the conference table, they'll probably have agendas in hand, because a well-executed agenda is viewed as an agreement and people want to verify compliance.

(A few words of caution: If on occasion a preliminary agenda is circulated while you wait to confirm or obtain information, don't send it off looking like the real thing.)

Agenda insurance is a little like health or property insurance. You want to know it's available but would prefer not to use it. On the meeting day that no agendas are distributed on the spot, take a bow. Your agenda has earned the respect it deserves.

Consider Your Seating Plan Carefully.

Seating can play an important role in shaping the tone as well as the substance of a meeting. Mark L. Knapp, author of books on nonverbal communication, argues that seating behavior is not random and that how people seat themselves has an effect on how the meeting proceeds. He also claims that communication tends to go back and forth between people rather than around a table.

If you want participants to sit quietly and listen, it might be wise to arrange chairs in a classroom configuration. If you want to encourage discussion and generate a sense of team spirit, use a round table with no obvious sides. A rectangular table tends to encourage dominant personalities to take charge by sitting on the ends or in the middle of one side, often the side with the fewest seats, Knapp maintains. It's also interesting to note that, according to research, placing naturally shy or nondominant personalities in positions of dominance—at the end of a table, for example—does not make them participate more.

A meeting should be neither a social event nor a battleground. Seat your participants in such a way that neither business alliances nor social cliques are reinforced. If this is a problem-solving meeting, avoid seating factions across a table from each other; however, if you want to present a strong united front to a client or competitor, group your forces facing the other participants. If anyone is to make a presentation, be sure that person is clearly visible and easily heard from his or her position.

Introduce the Participants.

In a discussion meeting, be sure that the names, positions, and areas of expertise of each participant are announced at the beginning of the meeting, either by you or by having each individual introduce himself or herself. This is more than common courtesy; it ensures that no participant is placed at a political disadvantage.

Establish the Rules.

If this meeting is to be governed by rules—company regulations, *Robert's Rules of Order,* your own rules—announce them at the outset and be sure that everyone understands them.

Get All the Facts or Ideas on the Table Before Evaluating Them.

It makes sense to introduce all the information before discussing or debating its merits. For example, if the purpose of the meeting is to generate a plan of action for the next quarter, ask for ideas without discussion until all ideas have been offered. Then debate the merits of each proposal. This approach both encourages people to volunteer ideas and prevents the meeting from bogging down in a discussion of the first proposal.

If background information or expertise is necessary to move the discussion along, it is the leader's responsibility to provide it. For example, if the discussion of a new computer software program requires knowledge of other comparable systems, it's up to you to provide that information or know who else in the room has it and call on that person for the information.

Keep the Ball Rolling.

It is up to you to keep the meeting moving forward. This can be done in a number of ways:

1. **Keep an eye on the clock.** Stick to the time allotted in the agenda to each item of discussion. Remember, a meeting is not necessarily democratic. You're the boss, and it's enough to say politely, "It's time we moved on; if we have time we'll return to this subject later."

2. **Know your questions in advance.** Part of your preparation for the meeting should be a list of questions to which you need answers. Knowing them in advance prevents your forgetting them in the course of the meeting.

3. **Keep the conversation relevant.** This is probably the single hardest task of a meeting leader and, in the interests of productivity, the most important. Again, remember that a meeting is not a democracy; on matters of running the meeting, no one gets to vote but you. Whenever a participant strays from the subject, a reminder is in order. Perhaps the question "Could you relate what you've just said to this particular situation?" will do the trick. Or a gentle "In the interest of time, I think we'd better get back to the subject at hand" may suffice.

4. **Summarize the proceedings as you go.** As leader, it's up to you to provide a summary of the discussion at regular intervals, preferably when switching from one subject to another. This helps participants organize their thoughts and keeps the discussion within a manageable framework.

Insist on Conclusions and Action.

At the end of the meeting, be sure that participants have arrived at a consensus. That consensus should include decisions made and actions to be taken. Summarize the group's conclusions, focusing on any actions decided upon. "It is my understanding that we have agreed that a new sales strategy is essential and that, in the next three weeks, each of you will draft an element of the plan as it pertains to your department. Is that how all of you see it?"

Be sure to review whatever assignments were given in the course of the meeting so that participants leave the room knowing exactly what their next step is.

Communicate with Class. Your communication skills help set the tone for the entire meeting, and your ability to express yourself well and to encourage others to do the same helps make the difference between a productive and an unproductive meeting.

Some pointers:

1. **Help others to express themselves well.** You can do this by asking for clarification when it's needed: "I understand you to mean . . . Have I got it right?" or by asking for a summary: "Could you summarize that point for me? I'm not sure I understand." In encouraging others to express themselves, be certain not to criticize their efforts. Saying "You don't make any sense; could you repeat that?" does little except embarrass the victim and encourage silence.

2. **Avoid editorializing.** As meeting leader, you are certainly entitled to your opinions. However, in the interest of generating a lively discussion in which all participants feel comfortable about expressing their opinions, it is essential that you clearly label your opinions as such: "My opinion on that matter is . . ." Otherwise, make every effort to keep your opinions out of the discussion. Phrase your questions, for example, in a neutral way. There's a world of difference between "Don't you think that idea is rather weak?" and "What do you think about the merits of that idea?"

3. Offer your colleagues the same courtesies you expect from them.
Rudeness, aside from bruising the feelings and often denting the
self-esteem of others, is unproductive. If you want the most out
of your meeting participants, treat them nicely! Look them in the
eye when talking to them; don't talk when they are talking; don't
leave the room for any reason without declaring a break in the
meeting; don't do other work while the meeting is in progress;
and hold all telephone calls.

On those occasions when one or more meeting participants
speak English as a second language, some additional courteous
behavior should be considered. Remember:

◆ People will probably require more time to read materials or
confer with translators. It may be that only a phrase or two is
unfamiliar and needs interpretation. Still, you may have to
halt proceedings briefly so this can be accomplished.

◆ Use of idioms may be confusing and clear communication
compromised as a result. When some meeting participants
pepper their comments with idioms, rephrase the comments.

Someone says, "Jim's team has knocked the socks off the competition with the new widget design."

You say, "You mean we're making more sales than our competi-
tors because of the new widget design?"

If you handle this with tact, no one will notice, except the individual who benefits from your clarification.

Body language may be subject to different interpretation, too. If
the other person won't look you in the eye, for example, it may
not be owing to disinterest or rudeness. Be aware of possible differences and don't jump to false conclusions.

Decision making can be influenced by cultural background as well as by an individual's personality traits. You risk robbing some people of their dignity if you press for a firm answer on a matter and don't provide any options. Just because you wouldn't react like that, don't assume the same is true of others. Courtesy dictates that you consider another's modus operandi and when appropriate be ready to make allowances.

4. **Make the most of your speaking voice.** Can everyone hear you? Is your speaking voice clear? Do you speak too quickly? Too slowly? Do you have a tendency to use a monotone or perhaps raise your intonation at the end of every sentence as though you were asking questions instead of making statements? It's practically impossible to communicate with class if you ignore what your speaking voice is and isn't doing! Pitch, pace, and vocal quality (e.g., relaxed or tense) are characteristics that should be scrutinized.

One way to improve your speaking voice is by joining an organization like Toastmasters International, Inc. [23182 Arroyo Vista, Rancho Santa Margarita, CA (949) 858-8255]. Members assist one another to get better and better at making oral presentations. Locate local chapters online at: *www.toastmasters.org*. Another approach is to join a community chorus or theater group. In addition to other benefits, you're practically guaranteed the opportunity to perfect your speaking voice.

A pleasing and effective speaking voice is a valuable asset, whether you're pursuing career excellence or sharing time with family and friends.

5. **Wow them with your powers of persuasion.** Earn bonus points at the meeting when you know what people want and let them have it. Aristotle said, "The fool tells me his reasons; the wise man

persuades me with my own." When you communicate with class, you expect to be effective. Model yourself after Aristotle's wise man and you'll find that the process is easier.

ILLUSTRATION: You want executives to authorize overtime for your department so you can meet seasonal deadlines. You anticipate disapproval because executives are focused on staying within budget guidelines. You rise at the meeting and acknowledge the importance of adhering to your department's budget. You carefully explain how it will be necessary to cut back on work hours shortly after the holiday season because it's now necessary to authorize overtime to meet seasonal demands.

Because people do not live by logic alone, appeal to your coworkers' emotions, too. Famed psychologist Carl Jung wrote, "There can be no transforming of darkness into light and of apathy into movement without emotion." Pride fuels emotion, so you extol the efforts of the various departments that resulted in an unexpected doubling of orders. (How could anyone have foreseen the need for overtime expense twelve months earlier when you prepared the budget?) Keep these key points in mind as you prepare to be persuasive, and you should get more of what you want.

Keep the Discussion Balanced.

As meeting leader, you face the task of seeing both sides, or as many sides as are presented, of the story. Whereas other participants may have a position to present or defend, your role in mediating the discussion is to balance the ideas and opinions. You can do this most effectively by recognizing one opinion and asking for others: "I understand what you're saying, George. Does anyone have a different approach?" *In order to make the most informed decision, it is best to consider as many viewpoints as possible.*

Break Up the Fights.

Healthy disagreement is one thing; fighting is another. It is your responsibility to maintain order in a meeting by insisting that all players stick to the rules and the subject under discussion. Any personal attacks must be stopped *immediately*.

Listen, Listen, Listen.

> *You go up to the counter of a fast-food restaurant and wait to get the attention of the teenager behind the register, who is chatting with his burger-flipping buddy. Finally he faces you and you say, "I'd like a double cheeseburger, small order of fries, and*

> *a small Coke." "Do you want fries with that?" he*
> *replies. "Yes," you say, "that's what I said." "What*
> *size drink do you want?" he asks.*

We are, alas, a nation of nonlisteners. The loss in revenues, profits, and productivity to businesses resulting from poor listening habits totals $1 billion a year, according to Dr. Lyman Steil, formerly a professor of rhetoric at the University of Minnesota. Dr. Steil is quoted in *American Salesman* magazine as saying that 80 percent of waking hours are involved in communication, only 45 percent of that time listening.

Your ability and willingness to listen is essential; they make the difference between a meeting that is efficiently conducted and that produces well-thought-out ideas and opinions and one that is not cost-effective and is marked by inconclusive results. So how do you learn to listen?

In the theater, actors are often given a "side," a card containing their lines but not the other actors', only the cue words signaling when it is time for the actor in question to speak. The result? The actor has to listen, because he or she has no idea when the cue will come or what the gist of the conversation preceding it is. The result, on stage, can be a heightened sense of natural conversation rather than of actors reciting memorized lines.

In the course of a meeting, participants, too, have no idea what others will say next. Unfortunately, we tend to be preoccupied with what *we* plan to say next, because we naturally want to look and sound our best. As meeting leader, you should make every effort to ask questions because you want to *hear* the answers. Train yourself to listen, assimilate what was said, and *then* respond. Have questions prepared in advance so you don't have to think of them while someone else is speaking. Practice will help you direct the flow of conversation easily, keep the discussion relevant, and provide a valuable framework of give and take within which other participants can work together to accomplish your goal.

Keep the Record Straight.

One of the simplest, and most often forgotten, steps in running a successful meeting is taking notes. Be sure that someone other than you, preferably someone with legible handwriting or a laptop computer, records the proceedings of your meeting. The minutes should detail, in outline form, all subjects discussed, any decisions reached, and relevant opinions and ideas offered during the discussion, including the participant who offered the idea. In choosing someone to take notes, it is advisable to pick someone who has no ax to grind—that is, someone who will record the proceedings without bias and without giving more or less weight to specific opinions, ideas, or decisions than they deserve.

Chapter 7

Encouraging Participation:

Wallflowers Have Ideas, Too

"Give your evidence," the King repeated angrily, "or I'll have you executed whether you are nervous or not."

—*Alice's Adventures in Wonderland*

Participation is the very soul of a meeting. There are, of course, briefings in which speeches by one or more individuals dominate the proceedings, but rarely is there a meeting of any kind that does not involve some give and take, some interaction of ideas and opinions.

A meeting that works is one in which all participants can express their thoughts without fear of ridicule or reprisal, secure in the knowledge that their contributions will be heard and taken seriously, if not always agreed with. Such an environment allows the most productive ideas to rise to the top, the result of a creative process involving conversation, disagreement, and, finally, consensus. You face no greater challenge in your role as meeting leader than to create this kind of atmosphere.

Much of the quality of the interaction in a meeting depends on you. It is your job to coax ideas from each participant, stimulate discussion, and guide the group to the decision-making stage (if that is the purpose of the meeting). Whether you succeed depends on two factors: the meeting environment you create and your skill at getting the most from your participants.

CREATING AN ATMOSPHERE FOR PARTICIPATION

Each of us is profoundly affected by the world around us, specifically by the people around us. Walk into a room full of angry people and you feel the tension; join a group celebrating a happy occasion and you feel the excitement. Take part in group meditation and you're apt to feel the serenity of the moment.

The same applies to the work environment. The Boss is tense and harried; you become tense and worried. The sales figures are up; everyone relaxes. Much of the quality of discussion and debate in your meeting depends on the energy and the personality you bring to it. If you arrive angry, tense, determined to prove a point, or suspicious, you're likely to have a roomful of mummies to contend with. In contrast, if your mood is relaxed, friendly, and unhurried, you are likely to have a roomful of talkers. It's up to you to set the tone of the meeting. These are some ways to go about it:

1. **Join the Meeting with an Open Mind.** Leave your preconceptions and assumptions behind and enter the meeting with a desire to learn, to find out, to hear what's happening.

2. **Start Off with a Smile and a Greeting.** You wouldn't think of meeting a group of friends without at least a "Hello!" Why should a meeting be any different?

3. **Respect the Differences Among People and Work with Them.** Like it or not, people's personalities differ: Some are loud and boisterous, others quiet as mice. Not everyone is easy to work with. But it's a lot easier to work *with* the differences than to try to change them to make yourself comfortable. Be prepared to accept those you find difficult, encourage those who are timid, and keep a healthy perspective with your friends. The ideal meeting is one in which everybody takes part; how well you accept the many personalities in the room helps determine how many are willing to play the game.

4. **Recognize Individual Expertise and Talent.** No one likes to be one of the herd, so give individuals a chance to shine. In the course of discussions, call on those you know have something of value to contribute. If there are a number of strangers in the crowd, it might be wise to ask, "Does anyone else here have some expertise or ideas on this subject?"

5. **Give Credit and Thanks Where They Are Due.** Nothing is more disheartening, particularly for junior members of the company, than to have their ideas and opinions appropriated by someone else. And it happens all the time. Rob the Rookie presents an idea to Sam the Supervisor, and by the time it gets to Grinch the Boss the idea has become Sam's. In many cases the switch is unintentional; in others it's deliberate. You can foster a sense of security and confidence in a meeting by being sure to acknowledge to the group your awareness and appreciation of someone's idea: "That's an

interesting idea, Rob; I like the way you think. Does anyone else have a comment on Rob's idea?"

6. **Accept the Challenge of Others.** As leader, you are in the hot seat. It's your responsibility to accept criticism of your ideas, even of the way you run the meeting, as long as the criticism is directed at your actions or opinions rather than at your person. If someone says, "You're a damned fool," a sharp rebuke is called for. But if the challenge is directed at your ideas, it's up to you to respond without getting defensive.

7. **Be Sincere.** Have you ever noticed how people have different personalities for the different roles they play? The change often happens when they're asked to take on new responsibilities. A colleague with whom you've joked and eaten chili dogs on the street gets promoted and suddenly starts wearing vests and talking in a deeper voice. Now he eats sushi, in restaurants. "I thought I knew that guy. Suddenly he's a different person," you

think to yourself. When you run a meeting, be yourself. After all, you're in a room with people who have the same kind of worries and fears that you have. The disguise takes too much energy, and in the end it won't fit right anyway. Let yourself show through; it's the best way to establish a productive working relationship.

8. Respond to Signals. Take the pulse of your meeting by responding to verbal and nonverbal signals that tell you what the participants are experiencing. In a back issue of *Meetings & Conventions,* Carl Camden, of Cleveland State University's Department of Communications, offers a checklist of signals and what they mean. Fidgeting and wandering eyes, for example, signal inattention; to counter such signals, you might ask questions or ask a participant to speak. Avoiding eye contact or raising voice pitch may mean the group members are anxious. Camden suggests you ask them directly what's troubling them. When discussions are unproductive, the group is likely to take on a defensive posture, making negative and exaggerated comments such as "That's dumb," or "You always do that." You can get things back on track by asking the most vocal participants to argue the other side or to listen to others without speaking for a few minutes, Camden says.

NOW SOME DON'TS:

1. Don't Dominate the Discussion. As much as you'd like to set the world straight on a few things, this is not the time to do so. Your role is to moderate the conversation, making sure everyone has equal time. A few ideas, an opinion or two, particularly when laying the groundwork for the discussion, are perfectly acceptable. Otherwise, bite your tongue and ask the questions.

2. Don't Harass the Witness. You may have the authority to make the meeting rules, but you don't have the power to change people's opinions (however wrong you know they are) or change personalities. You can't badger someone into offering an opinion, and you shouldn't humiliate someone into holding his tongue.

3. **Don't Interrupt (with Exceptions).** "Do unto others as you would have them do unto you" holds true in running a meeting. Politeness goes a long way in accomplishing your task of encouraging everyone to participate. An interruption, except in the case of a particularly long-winded speaker who lost sight of the subject minutes ago, is an unnecessary insult.

4. **Don't Get Personal.** However strongly you disagree with someone, no matter how exasperated you are at that someone's behavior, ad hominem attacks are unproductive. There are better ways of encouraging a wallflower to speak than by saying, "I know you're real shy, but don't you have something to offer?" It's desirable to

accept the wide range of personalities in the room but quite unacceptable to bring those personalities into the conversation.

5. Don't Insist on Participation Simply for the Sake of Participation. It would be nice if everyone felt comfortable speaking in front of others, but the fact is, not everyone does. If, after gentle prodding, a member of the group is still obviously happier as a silent partner, don't push. Offer that person, and all the others, the opportunity to communicate any thoughts to you in private or on paper. At the end of the meeting you might say, "I'll be available in my office if anyone wants to discuss any of this further. Or jot down your thoughts and drop them off when you have the chance. But don't waste time—we have to move on this in a hurry."

6. Don't Embarrass Yourself with Bad Humor. A sense of humor is a terribly personal thing; one person's joke is another person's insult. There's certainly room for good humor, but a meeting is rarely a place for jokes. If you want your audience to have a laugh, make yourself the object: "A funny thing happened to me on the way to this meeting . . ."

GETTING THE MOST FROM THE GROUP

Creating the right atmosphere for participation in a meeting is more than half the battle; people who feel comfortable and secure will *want* to share their thoughts or opinions. There are, however, a number of ways you can build on that success to maximize the quality of the group's interaction.

1. Act As If You *Expect* Everyone to Participate. From the outset, let it be known (by making eye contact, smiling, keeping your comments brief, asking questions) that this meeting is for discussion, not speeches.

2. **Ask the Right Questions.** The goal of questioning in a meeting should be to get people to talk, to elaborate, to explain, or to theorize; in other words, to feel comfortable about expressing themselves fully and honestly. Structuring your questions in the right way can help. Never ask a question that requires only a "yes" or "no" unless all you want is a vote. Ask for opinions and speculations; ask difficult questions based on the group's expertise. Don't sound condescending or hostile. Be sure your questions are clearly phrased and easily understood; they should be short and to the point.

3. **Look for Opportunities to Include as Many People as Possible in the Discussion.** Let it be known that contrasting opinions are welcome. As one person finishes a comment, turn to the group and ask, "Does anyone else have an idea on that?"

4. **Take Every Opportunity to Expand the Subject.** One useful method of drawing new speakers into the discussion is by stretching the subject to include new thoughts and facts through remarks such as, "That's very interesting. I wonder if we could carry it further or apply it in other ways. Does anyone else care to comment on that?" or, "I like that idea. Do you think we could apply it to the idea we were discussing a minute ago?"

5. Use the Group's Expertise and Talents to Increase Participation. It's always nice to be recognized for having a skill or knowledge, and a smart leader knows that acknowledging an individual's expertise is a good way to draw that person into a discussion: "George, I understand you've done some work in this field. Are we on the right track here? What's your opinion?"

A WORD ABOUT CONFLICT

One of the most difficult aspects of human interaction is learning to disagree without fighting. Conflicting opinions, for most of us, all too quickly become "conflict." In family life, the disagreement may escalate to flying pots and pans. In office life, for the most part, the anger triggered by a difference of opinion festers as resentment and suspicion. To avoid such difficult situations, many of us sometimes go to unnecessary extremes to avoid any sign of disagreement.

Conflict is OK. While you may hope it doesn't occur, you should not be afraid of it. No one said that everything about a meeting has to be cheerful. Strong disagreement is bound to generate a few emotions. It can generate some sound thinking as well—but only in a controlled environment. It's up to you as meeting leader to maintain that control.

The best way to maintain control is by insisting that all parties stick to the subject at hand and refrain from personal remarks. By restricting the boundaries of disagreement to one subject, you force participants to leave the larger, emotion-packed issues—the hidden personal agendas—out of the discussion and minimize the risk of inappropriate outbursts. It's not always pleasant playing referee, but sometimes it's unavoidable.

Chapter 8

Handling the
Tough Ones:

Dealing with Difficult Situations

"Curiouser and curiouser," cried Alice.

—*Alice's Adventures in Wonderland*

No one promised that running a meeting would be a piece of cake, and from time to time you are bound to encounter tough situations and difficult people. Participants who won't stop talking, people who have nothing to say and spend hours saying it, angry people and stubborn people, squabblers and tyrants—these are some of the characters you're likely to encounter. Then there are the meetings that won't fly, and the black holes. With a little practice, however, you'll learn to negotiate your way through even the toughest challenges. There are a couple of general rules that can and should be applied to all the challenges you are likely to run up against.

All Problems Are "People" Problems; Approach Them from That Perspective.

A blown fuse on the slide projector is easily remedied: just replace the fuse. But, except for a mechanical breakdown, the problems that affect meetings are caused by people, and you can't simply throw out the problem and start over. People problems are driven by egos, insecurities, ambitions, moods, likes and dislikes, and personalities. However unproductive that blowhard across the room is—the one who has monopolized the conversation with irrelevant remarks—telling him to put a sock in it may only create a new problem. Bearing this in mind will help you find the appropriate solution without creating new difficulties.

Keep Personalities and Value Judgments Out of the Solution.

In moments of frustration, it is often tempting to offer assumptions, evaluations, or opinions as the reason for someone else's shortcoming: "If you didn't waste so much time, you would have finished that assignment," or, "If you weren't so stubborn, you'd see the other side of the question." In resolving problems during a meeting, keep personalities out of the solution. Deal with the problem; forgo your opinions about why it exists, however right they may be. There is no place for embarrassment or humiliation in the work environment, and personal comments are at best unproductive, because they further alienate the recipient. Stick to the facts: If the work was not done, what can be done to resolve that problem? Or, a particular individual is unable, or unwilling, to see both sides of an issue; what can be done to help him see differently?

"Avoid personalities and focus on problems and process. It's all right to get emotional about an issue, but keep it from becoming a personal attack." This is one important point mentioned in a business-meeting article online at *www.dealconsulting.com*. Jack Deal, company founder, earned his bachelor's degree in behavioral psychology from Harvard University. Another point: "Start the meeting with something light. Humor makes everyone relaxed."

HANDLING DIFFICULT SITUATIONS

The first question to be answered in finding solutions to difficult situations is, "When is a problem a problem?" The answer is simple:

> *A problem is any action or condition that serves to prevent you, as meeting leader, from accomplishing your purpose.*

Distraction, delay, obstacle, inertia, boredom, inappropriate emotions—any of these can be a problem if it prevents the meeting from moving forward.

What follows are some of the most common difficulties you are likely to encounter and some possible approaches to resolving them.

The Yakkers.

These are the people who sit across the room and, heads together, carry on a whispered conversation while the rest of the group is either listening to a speaker or attempting to discuss an idea. Nothing is louder than a whisper in this situation; quickly heads turn, the speaker stumbles, and if not nipped in the bud, one whisper generates others and the meeting grinds to a halt.

One solution is to stop the meeting momentarily to let the whisperers finish their conversation or at least get the message that you would appreciate their silence. A glance in their direction might also serve the purpose; as a last resort, you might ask one of the culprits if he or she has anything to add to what is being discussed.

The Interminables.

These are the well-intentioned people who, though they have many ideas to contribute, tend to go on and on and on without any organization to their thoughts and with a great deal of repetition.

Look for an appropriate moment to politely break into these monologues. Thank the speaker for his or her ideas, recognize their value, and then shift the focus to someone else. "George, I wonder if I might interrupt for a moment. I'm interested in that idea, and I wonder if anyone else has a comment on it."

The Vacuums.

From time to time you will encounter an individual who is firmly convinced that he has volumes to contribute, whereas in fact his comments are irrelevant to any discussion and serve only to shift the focus away from the work to be done.

At first you might try guiding such a person back to the subject with questions. If this does not work, and it probably won't, the only solution may be to ignore him as politely as possible. This can be done by calling on other speakers and, seemingly accidentally, overlooking his requests to talk.

The Squabblers.

These are the fighters, those unhappy individuals who need to take on the world, sometimes quite offensively. In a meeting situation they disagree with every idea proposed and belittle other participants. There is simply no room in a meeting for this kind of behavior.

First of all, be aware that such an individual is using the meeting situation to express fears and emotions that have nothing to do with the current situation. There is no use confronting such an individual about emotions. Questions about anger or abusiveness will only be met with denial.

You may try to rally group consensus against the squabbler's approach in the hope that prevailing odds will quiet him. "George thinks we are wasting our time, that this is a ridiculous idea. Do the rest of you agree?" It is also perfectly appropriate to ask the individual to stop the behavior. Do so directly and calmly, without adding any personal opinion about his character. "George, I think those kinds of comments are preventing us from accomplishing what we've set out to do. I would appreciate it if you would refrain from making them." If all else fails, ask him to leave the meeting and suggest a private conference with you later in the day.

The Mules.

Few people are more exasperating than the individual who clings to an idea and argues for it relentlessly. Long after the topic of conversation has changed, there she is, raising her pet issue again and again. She slows the progress of the meeting, delays decisions, and serves as a thorn in the side of other participants.

When it becomes obvious that this is a person with a mission, let her state her case and then politely avoid her. If she succeeds in raising the topic once again, find the opportunity to settle the matter by involving the rest of the group. Thank her for her idea and ask several others for contrasting views. If she persists, put the matter to a vote. "Mary feels strongly that this is the best way to go on this project. I'd like to see a show of hands of those who agree with her."

The Tyrants.

Tyrants are those characters who have an opinion about everything. They never shut up. Whatever the subject, they're experts. Their effect on a meeting is like that of chlorine in a swimming pool: They kill every sign of life.

Once again, politely ignoring that waving, frantic hand may help. But tyrants may have valuable contributions to make, however offensively they make them. Try to keep their comments as brief as possible. Find a moment to interrupt, recognize what has been said by rephrasing it or summarizing the main points, and then let the group know that you would like its involvement as well: "George, that's an interesting viewpoint, but I'd really like to hear some others. Would anyone else care to comment?" The key to taming The Tyrant is matching his output with other speakers.

The Lost Souls.

The meeting has been under way for forty-five minutes, and in wanders The Lost Soul. "Sorry I'm late," she says, and then she does one of two things: "Where are we?" she asks. "Can someone bring me up to date?"; or she proceeds to jump into the conversation, eloquently arguing points that were discussed long before she arrived. At best The Lost Soul is a distraction, throwing the conversation momentarily into reverse.

Deal with this one quickly by saying, "I'll fill you in at the break, Mary." Draw her attention to the printed agenda and whatever background or collateral materials have been distributed and suggest, "Take a look through those while we finish up this topic."

The Bosses.

This can be the deadliest situation of all. Your meeting is in full swing. Ideas are flying, the enthusiasm is high, when in walks The Boss. A second later she says, "I know you are the experts in this matter, but it seems to me the best idea would be . . ." Suddenly, the enthusiasm is gone; the ideas have vanished. Who can argue with The Boss? Now there is more concern about looking good and sounding smart than throwing ideas against the wall.

What to do? Throw her out? Hardly. But you can be firm, and you can trust your own judgment. Don't hesitate to reinforce the contributions already made by the group members: "Before you came in, we came up with some ideas that I think are worth considering." Give credit to individuals for their contributions to the meeting. Keep control of the meeting; she may be The Boss, but it's your show. Respond to her comments by asking for other ideas *without* asking the other participants to comment on The Boss's contribution.

The Silence.

Much like a Stephen King horror novel, this situation can strike terror in the heart of a meeting leader. You bounce into the meeting, enthusiasm at a peak, throw out the first few questions or topics, and what happens? Nothing. The room is silent. Eyes stare at note pads, throats are cleared, feet shuffle, and no one says a word.

What can you do? First of all, try to determine the problem. Is the group prepared? Do the participants need more information? Is it clear what you're asking for? Have you somehow cowed them? Then start again: "Let's backtrack a minute, because I'd like you all to understand what we have to do here today." Begin with the agenda, making clear what you intend to discuss. Ask if everyone received the background materials and if there are any questions. Finally, you do the talking for a while. Give the group the chance to size you up and get a feel for your style and your expectations. Then single out specific individuals to answer questions rather than throwing the question to the group as a whole.

The Wall.

This is the moment when everything grinds to a halt; the group is deadlocked and going in circles. The same arguments are raised and refuted again and again. The Wall is a waste of time and needs to be broken down quickly.

Take charge by summarizing the arguments or ideas for the group. Don't ask for clarification or agreement, and then put the matter to a vote. Conclude the proceedings: "I think we've covered the subject pretty well. As I understand it, these are our options. The time has come to decide. How many are in favor of . . ." If the situation does not call for a vote, perhaps the issue can be left with a summary and a further assignment: "This is the way I see our discussion. By next week I'd like each of you to come up with three solutions to the problem." The key to breaking down The Wall is shifting the process from discussion to action.

If all efforts to break a deadlock fail, it may be advisable to end the meeting and schedule another, preferably with a different cast of characters, so that the same deadlock is not repeated.

The Black Hole.

The Black Hole is a case of terminal boredom. The crowd is listless, restless, and unproductive. Whispered conversations break out across the room, bodies slip out to the rest rooms, papers rustle, and faces stare blankly at the ceiling. Not an atmosphere conducive to accomplishing your goal.

Make a quick mental review of the situation. Have you exhausted the topic? Are you not making yourself clear? Do you need a break? Do you need to lighten up? Whatever the problem, the first step, in most cases, is a break. If more work must be accomplished, first give everyone a chance to shift gears, refresh themselves, maybe even go out of the room and gripe about your handling of the meeting. When the meeting resumes, restate the group's position with respect to the subject under discussion. Help the players to make a personal connection to the subject. Be sure that they understand its significance in relation to the company's larger operations and help them see where their individual role fits in.

THE STAFF MEETING

Probably the most common of all business meetings, staff meetings are often the deadliest as well. You'd think, with all the practice, that we'd have gotten it right by now. In fact, staff meetings are too often boring and unproductive. Why?

The most likely reason is that staff meetings are usually taken for granted, by the participants as well as the leader. Because most happen routinely and according to company policy, they are often poorly prepared and without purpose.

If your company policy calls for regular staff meetings whether they are needed or not, the least you can do is make it productive. Be sure that the meeting each week has a stated purpose that requires some kind of action. It's not enough to say, "OK, let's hear what you guys have been doing. Fine, good-bye." At the end of each meeting, hand out assignments: "George, by next week I want you to have done A, B, and C, and be ready to report on the results."

Keep staff meetings short; there's no reason why the department's business cannot be taken care of in half an hour. Add some variety: Change the meeting's location, if possible, or surprise the group with different refreshments each week. Most of all, use the opportunity of a staff meeting to reward and encourage as well as make assignments: "I'm very pleased with the work you did on Project X, George. Congratulations," or, "Kathy, your writing is coming along very well. If you need more help, let me know." With very little effort on your part, the deadly staff meeting can become an important motivational tool, as well as a communications device.

> *When dealing with difficult situations, learn from your experience. After each meeting, take time to review the problem areas.*

◆ What was my role?

◆ What did I do right?

◆ What could I have done differently?

◆ What are my strengths and weaknesses in handling that particular situation?

Answer those questions, jot down your answers for safekeeping, and you'll find that handling difficult people and tough situations will soon become a manageable, even challenging, part of running a productive meeting.

Chapter 9

Collateral Materials:

Reinforcement Rather than Distraction

The Fish-Footman began by producing from under his arm a great letter, nearly as large as himself.

—*Alice's Adventures in Wonderland*

A dozen people sit around a large conference table. In front of each person is a stack of papers, charts, and reports. Some are reading, some have dropped their materials on the floor, one holds a chart up to the light, and still others are rustling through their stacks. The leader of the meeting is making a presentation, but is soon interrupted with, "Excuse me, where are we in this report?" What's wrong here? A valuable meeting tool is being misused.

Collateral materials or handouts can be a fine addition to a meeting, but all too often they serve merely to distract and to slow the proceedings. As a meeting leader, one of your important tasks is learning how and when to use printed materials to increase the productivity of your meeting.

Follow this simple rule:

> *Collateral materials should provide necessary information, clarify a discussion, or reinforce a point; they should never become the subject of the meeting.*

Good collateral materials are relevant to the subject being discussed and are easily understood without disrupting the flow of conversation.

What are collateral materials? Collaterals are any kind of printed matter that is given to participants before, during, or after a meeting. A printed agenda, workbooks or worksheets, questionnaires and surveys, charts, written reports, statistics, news clips, marketing or sales plans, speeches, proposals, press kits and press releases—these can all be collateral material.

The first question to answer is whether to use collateral materials. The answer is yes, if you need to; no, if you plan to use them as a substitute for adequate preparation; yes, if they will lend support to your ideas or position; no, if they will distract your colleagues from what you have to say.

If you feel that reinforcement is necessary, there are several rules that, if followed, will help you make collaterals a valuable addition to your meeting.

1. **Allow Plenty of Time for Planning.** It takes time to prepare printed materials. They must be written, often designed, printed, and distributed. Be sure you coordinate your plans with everyone involved in the preparation process—writers, designers, editors, printers, mailroom staff—so that no link is missing. Also, let the meeting participants know what materials you plan to distribute so that duplication is avoided and everyone knows what to expect. If you've decided to distribute the materials in advance of the meeting, be sure to allow enough time for delivery and reading. A useful tool is a written timetable detailing exactly when each piece of material will be completed, the date of distribution, and names of those people receiving the material.

2. **Collaterals Should Be Written in Outline Form, Using as Few Words as Possible.** This is especially true if they are to be used during the meeting. A simplified form minimizes the distribution factor by allowing participants to concentrate on what is being said instead of reading the material. Materials to be distributed after the meeting may cover the topic in greater detail.

3. **If Thorough Reading of a Document Is Necessary to the Conduct of the Meeting, Be Sure Participants Have It Well Before the Date of the Meeting.** Do not read a document in its entirety during a meeting, no matter how important; it is a waste of everyone's time. You may assume that it has been read (if you distributed it in time) and simply summarize its contents during the meeting.

4. **"Walking" the Group Through a Report or Presentation Is Ineffective and Often Irritating.** A common practice, "walking" your audience through a document means leading them, page by page, through a report of some kind. Too often this technique masks a lack of preparation or lack of confidence on the part of the presenter. The process itself is distracting, as everyone fumbles with pages.

If you want to make a written presentation, let the audience read it before joining the meeting; the meeting itself should be devoted to an oral presentation that is reinforced by the report.

5. **Collateral Material Should Be the Subject of a Meeting Only if It Is the Subject of the Meeting.** If you are presenting a new ad campaign to a client, it is understandable that photographs, printed material, slides, and videos will be the topic of discussion. But only in cases when the visual media are the message should printed materials be the focus of the meeting. Otherwise, collaterals should complement the oral presentation or discussion.

6. **Make Use of Computer-Generated and Other Audiovisual Equipment to Minimize the Use of Printed Materials.** Charts, graphs, and statistics may be vital to the conduct of your meeting. If so, it may be better to display them through use of audiovisual devices than to distribute a printout to each participant during the meeting. This minimizes the distraction factor and helps focus the attention of the entire group.

7. **When Possible, Distribute Collateral Materials After the Meeting.** There may be occasions when you need to give out materials for use during the meeting. (The agenda is one item that must always be handed out as the meeting starts.) In general, however, hand out materials during the meeting only if they are essential to the conduct of business or if they significantly enhance your position. If they are repetitions or summaries of the oral presentation or discussion, they are best given out after the meeting so they do not serve as a distraction.

8. **Material Prepared for Background Should Be Clearly and Comprehensively Written.** Any documents prepared to be distributed before or after a meeting—reports, speeches, press kits or releases, proposals—should cover all the major elements of the topic in a self-explanatory fashion. Remember, the reader will not be able to ask you questions. The material should follow the sequence in which the topic is discussed in the meeting, and only relevant information should be included.

9. **As Meeting Leader, Maintain Control of What Materials Will Be Handed Out.** Be sure that you discuss with all other meeting participants what materials are to be distributed. This helps you set the tone for the meeting and enables you to eliminate any materials that are counterproductive to your goals.

Chapter 10

Audiovisual Assistance:

Enhancement Rather than Clutter

Take care of the sense, and the sounds will take care of themselves.

—*Alice's Adventures in Wonderland*

At a recent monthly meeting of a local Kiwanis Club, an area businessman was invited to talk about the challenge of keeping a major grocery store stocked with fresh fish, fruit, and vegetables. The speaker was a kindly sort who was well known in the community for his warmth and sense of humor.

The businessman had brought his slides with him, and his talk began with shots of a large truck on its way to the Boston markets in the wee hours of the morning. As he warmed up to the subject, the slides came faster and faster. And then one appeared upside down, and his listeners tilted their heads to look at a swordfish from Vietnam. Then there was a picture of the businessman's grandchildren, and he digressed a moment to discuss their schooling and latest feats of bravery and then went back to vegetables. The presentation continued in this fashion—the occasional slide aslant or reversed, more shots of the kids, a few of his trip to Europe—and a good time was had by all.

This example illustrates the basic rule for using audiovisual elements in a meeting: Whatever you use should enhance the presentation and not distract from it. Slides of your grandchildren or grandparents and shots of the family vacation are certainly inappropriate in most business meetings, but, intentionally or otherwise, in a less formal setting such as the local Kiwanis meeting they served to create an image for the speaker—that of a generous, friendly soul who, by the way, is one hell of a businessman as well.

Properly used in a meeting, visuals can accomplish many things. They can reinforce the key points of a presentation; lend an air of glamor or style to a meeting; generate a specific image or tone; enhance understanding; help convince the viewer; and move the presentation along by dividing it into highly visible units or sections. Visuals can also help speakers organize their thoughts and structure their presentation.

However, visuals can be distracting and confusing and can create a false or misguided impression or image for you or your company. To be effective, visuals should always play a supporting role, reinforcing your position, ideas, or goals; they should never overshadow or distort them.

CHOOSING A MEDIUM

The variety of visual aids available for use in meetings is staggering. There are slides, films, videos, television shows, audio presentations, overhead projections, blackboards, easels, charts, photographs, and three-dimensional displays. Computer-generated visual-aids programs such as Microsoft PowerPoint® are popular. They enable users to create slides with text graphics and special effects. The process can be so user-friendly it's easy to get carried away. Visual aids should enhance but not overwhelm presentations.

Don't overlook the value of CD-ROMs. They're computer disks with content that can't be altered (i.e., read-only memory). And, consider using DVDs, digital versatile disks that can hold about 133 minutes' worth of fine-quality video and audio material.

You can affix printouts to flip charts and posters or make a sufficient number of copies to use as handouts. It's important, however, to keep computer-generated material simple. Graphs and diagrams should support a single point and be easy to decipher. Information-dense material frustrates meeting attendees when they don't have time to deal with it.

Another computer resource you can turn to for targeted data is the Internet. The Internet enables you to literally reach out to the world to locate pertinent and timely information that you can present in a visual format.

Conference calls and video satellite transmissions are used to multiply the effectiveness of key company executives. The chief executive officer, who is based in California, for example, can be visible to and talk with company employees meeting in a New York office.

Your choice of visual aids will depend on several factors: the atmosphere you wish to create, the type of meeting you have planned, and how you intend to use audiovisuals to supplement your presentation. The key word is *supplement*. Supplement your presentation as opposed to "deliver" your presentation.

For a briefing in which one or more speakers will stand before an audience, you may decide on a slide presentation, film, or video. For a sales presentation or new business pitch, you may combine video, computers, slides, charts, and photo displays. For a training session, you may need only charts and graphs.

Each piece of equipment or concept has its own strengths and weaknesses.

The medium should match the occasion. Because computer-generated visual aids are trendy, anything less may disappoint your audience. For example, an engineering firm in New York recently created a state-of-the art, three-dimensional computer model to bid on the contract to rebuild a major part of the city's subway system. Flip charts or overhead transparencies in that situation would have seemed archaic.

The use of audiovisuals in a meeting requires a three-step process: organization, preparation, and implementation.

1. **Organization.** To organize the audiovisual component of your meeting, first decide on your reason for including it in your presentation. Do you want to create a dazzling, forceful image, or do you need a working tool to conduct a discussion? Is cost a factor? Does your budget restrict your use of expensive equipment or the preparation of slides, tapes, or displays?

   Then list all the materials you will need and how long it will take to obtain or prepare them. Don't forget to allow enough time to prepare overhead transparencies, slides, or videos. If you plan to engage a professional to create your visuals, try to give him or her as much time as possible; the more time he or she has to work with, the less costly it may be. If you need something tomorrow, be prepared to pay for it.

2. **Preparation.** The preparation stage may be handled by your staff, an outside firm, or a combination of the two. Allow yourself enough time to collect all the information that will go on the transparencies or slides. It is sound business practice to create an audiovisual checklist, separate from your meeting preparation checklist, on which you include all material to be produced and a list of all equipment to be used. Be sure that each deadline is met and confirmed.

3. **Implementation.** Implementing the audiovisual component of the meeting, of course, depends on what equipment you have chosen to use. Be certain, before the meeting, that the room to be used is

equipped properly and that the seating is arranged so that all participants can see the visuals. Make sure that the equipment is near enough to an electrical outlet so that you don't have to reorganize the room after everyone has arrived. If you are meeting in a hotel or someone else's office, be sure you know whom to contact in case of technical failure. Finally, don't try to do everything yourself. It is often most convenient for the speaker to use a remote when using a slide projector during a presentation, but you shouldn't have to run back and forth between VCR and podium or attempt to manipulate an overhead projector if the task simply involves changing transparencies. If you do use an assistant, have a rehearsal; be certain that the assistant is familiar with the equipment and its use as well as with the sequence of materials to be shown. The assistant also should be familiar with your presentation so that you don't have to pause repeatedly to call out for a new picture.

Always bear in mind the old saying, "A picture is worth a thousand words." Like it or not, you will be judged by the audiovisuals you choose. Even your choice of colors will have an effect. Be certain that they, and all your visuals, convey an image that is appropriate to the event, the company, and you. This is why corporations spend millions developing a logo, why the advertising industry is alive and well, and why image consultants get paid big bucks. It is nice to believe that intelligence, expertise, and the ability to communicate are the qualities by which we are perceived, but the fact is that, if an impression has to be made quickly (as in a meeting), a visual impression has the most influence. For that reason, as you consider the use of visuals in your next meeting, remember that having no visual presentation at all may be more productive than having an ill-conceived one.

A STOP SIGN

Here's a different way a visual aid can support meeting success. If you suspect the meeting may generate finger pointing and negative criticism, use a visual aid like a traffic stop sign.

Why not use a red board to announce what won't be discussed? Position it where everyone can see it. If feasible, design it to look like a traffic stop sign. Most folks will get the message fast.

"We were there to generate ideas and enthusiasm about the quality process and move it forward," said a company director who used a stop-sign-type visual aid.

She placed a black felt board at the front of the conference room. It stated the purpose of the meeting, gave some facts, and featured a statement about what wouldn't be discussed.

"We moved quickly and effectively," the director reported. The visual information acted as a silent yet constant reminder that this wasn't a forum for negative criticism, and it contributed to the meeting's success.

Chapter 11

Guest Speakers Are Welcome:

Outsiders Can Motivate and Inspire

"We can talk," said Tiger-Lily, "when there's anybody worth talking to."

—*Alice's Adventures in Wonderland*

An exciting guest speaker adds sparkle to a meeting. The right guest speaker can motivate, inspire, educate, or do all three.

If you associate guest speakers with large gatherings, it's time to think small. There's no reason why you can't invite a guest speaker to your next any-size meeting, and reap the benefits.

You may want to invite a guest speaker when

The project or group lacks energy and obviously needs a boost!
When people typically waltz into meetings with ho-hum attitudes, you'll want a speaker who delivers with enthusiasm. A high energy level tends to be contagious. Moreover, an outsider represents an

unknown element and the promise of something new. Because people find this alluring, the presence of a guest adds pizzazz to the occasion before a word is spoken.

You'd prefer not to say something but you know it must be said.
An outsider with pertinent credentials can say some things and be well received, whereas if you say them, you invite ill will. If, for example, too many office supplies are walking out the door with employees, but no one sees it for what it is—theft—a business security expert or antitheft consultant can set the record straight.

You want people to know they have a coveted place in the information loop.
You may be able to report with accuracy all of Jones's findings when he returned from the western regional conference, but if Jones speaks to the group, each person may think the information is more relevant because it comes from the source. It may be only a matter of perception, but that affects results. In this case, your guest speaker would be Jones.

You want to reach out to coworkers in other departments.
Inviting someone to speak is a form of flattery. As a result, your invitation fulfills a public relations task, but it also opens a fresh approach to communication. Not only are you taking care of your internal customers when you utilize this forum, but you beef up information channels. Don't be surprised if the invitation is reciprocated—you may be asked to be a guest speaker, too.

WHERE TO LOOK
The first place to look for a speaker is in your own backyard. If you don't find the speaker you want within the company, consider these resources:

◆ Suppliers. Goods or service providers may employ experts in a particular field of interest who are ready, willing, and able to speak at your meeting.

◆ A speakers bureau. Use an Internet search engine, such as *www.google.com,* to locate speakers. Try key words *professional speakers,* and you'll probably be inundated with information. Your industry association may operate a speakers bureau. Find out. If your company is based in or near a large city, check the telephone book for speakers bureau listings. Are you prepared to pay speakers' fees or expenses such as travel and lodging costs? You'll save time by narrowing your search if your budget is small or nonexistent.

◆ Professors from a nearby university whose area of expertise meshes with your meeting subject.

◆ A file you maintain when you attend community gatherings, training programs, or any event where an excellent speaker appears. (Speakers' business cards are readily available and can be maintained in this file.)

◆ Government offices. Speakers are available through many government agencies and affiliates. Personnel at these offices may also be able to arrange for the loan of audiovisual aids and other useful material.

◆ Ask the reference librarian in your community's main library for assistance in locating speakers from government groups and private associations.

AUDITION IN PROGRESS

When you contact an individual to discuss the possibility of him or her addressing your gathering, listen carefully to how this person speaks. If you're not face to face, you can't do much more than listen. Of course, you may not want to move ahead and extend an invitation until you've met the person. It's perfectly permissible to ask the potential speaker to stop by and say hello. Don't commit yourself to extending the invitation unless you believe this person will be an effective speaker.

You may want to ask if you can be in the audience when this person speaks to another group; or you may want to ask for references. Make one or two phone calls and ask these references specific questions, such as the following:

If ten is tops and five is adequate, what numerical rating would you give to Sally Smith's overall performance when you heard her speak? Did you get favorable feedback from listeners? If not, is that usual? Did Ms. Smith use good examples when she spoke? Can you remember two or more points she made?

Of course, you don't want to take too much of someone's time when he is acting as a reference. Still, you want to do your homework.

If an individual has a monotone voice, lacks enthusiasm, doesn't smile, speaks too quickly, talks a lot but says little, or in any way demonstrates that she isn't the speaker you want at your meeting—stop. Don't extend the invitation.

Of course, when you find a guest speaker who will be an asset, set the date.

WHO ARE YOU?

The guest speaker is the one who can best answer questions about himself. Accordingly, he can supply you with material for the introduction you must make before this individual speaks. Ask and you shall receive. Most speakers are delighted to oblige.

Feel free to tailor remarks to conform to your time constraints and focus on immediate goals. Because the introduction is a selling tool, however, don't subtract the sizzle and serve only the steak.

If you delegated the search for a speaker to someone else, why not ask that individual to make the introduction? You'll be giving credit where credit is due, which should assure that future searches are conducted in the most conscientious manner.

LET THE SPEAKER BE AWARE

A good speaker will prepare a beginning, a middle, and an end that conforms to a specific time allotment. You'll want to discuss time parameters in advance and stick to the plan, or the speaker will work at a disadvantage. An otherwise terrific presentation, for example, falls short when the ending must be rushed or abbreviated. It's not impractical to ask for a short presentation (i.e., twenty to thirty minutes) with a brief question and answer session to follow. A longer program probably doesn't belong in the meeting environment.

A good speaker should know something about the audience. If, for example, engineers and technical specialists are listening to the speaker, they'll relate best to information that's specific to their work. The speaker may want to use examples that spotlight project management challenges or electronic tools. Moreover, the speaker will want to delete information that's too elementary for this crowd. Unlike presentations that are designed for a broad audience, this presentation can and should be especially relevant to this particular group.

BE PREPARED

You'll want to know if the speaker has material to hand out, will need a table available for a flip chart, or has other needs. It may be that something as simple as an electric extension cord will be required. If you aren't prepared, there can be an awkward and unnecessary delay.

SIMPLE COURTESIES

When the speaker comes from outside the company, you'll want to make sure the guest is greeted properly upon arrival and escorted to the meeting room. If she needs assistance with slide projectors or other apparatuses, you'll want to be gracious and see to it that help is at hand. Some assistance may be necessary when the speaker departs, too. Because the speaker may enter or exit while the meeting is in progress, it will be necessary to plan ahead, so that the speaker's coming and going is orderly.

Unless there are unusual circumstances, the speaker should arrive before the meeting is called to order. If she arrives while the meeting is in progress, the interruption becomes a disruption, and that's not an auspicious way to make an entrance.

You may want to discuss privileged information at this meeting without the guest in the room; or the speaker may want to leave immediately after her appearance and you can discuss it then. It's easy to take a five-minute break while the speaker exits. If individuals are stimulated by what they've just heard, it gives them an opportunity to talk about it with a colleague, and thus the exit time is time well spent.

A DEPARTURE

Although you may not typically serve coffee and tea at meetings, you may want to depart from the norm when a guest speaker is present. Light refreshments served when the speaker concludes provides an opportunity for some one-on-one conversation. If the guest stays to talk to your colleagues and coworkers, good things can result. Some questions are raised only in private, and the tête-à-tête may also elicit an off-the-record answer that would otherwise be unspoken.

In addition, if your guest speaker is well known, you may not be forgiven if you don't allow time for each person to shake hands with the speaker. (Don't flirt with your boss's disapproval either by neglecting to invite her to stop by and say hello.)

When you're thinking about whether the speaker should be invited to speak first, last, or somewhere in the middle, consider the mix-and-mingle angle. If you know the speaker is able to stay and visit and if you believe this could be beneficial, conduct other meeting business before you introduce the speaker. Of course, a guest speaker's appearance could be the only item on the agenda. Consider this option if a prized guest speaker isn't able to conform to your meeting time schedule.

EVALUATING SPEAKERS

If the guest speaker idea catches fire in your circles, you may want to call for a written evaluation from meeting attendees after a speaker appears. If you maintain a file pertaining to excellent speakers you've heard at community meetings and elsewhere, that file is a natural place to maintain evaluations. It becomes another useful tool to use when starting a speaker search.

Keep the evaluation simple. Make it easy to fill out and return. If appropriate, circulate a single-page questionnaire the same way you route magazines and newsletters. You won't generate extra paper, and anyone will be able to see at a glance what people think about this speaker. Or ask people to rate the speaker immediately following the meeting before they leave the room. A simple form makes it easy to comply with this request.

Here's an example of a speaker evaluation form:

Speaker:
SAM SMITH

Topic:
HOW IMPROVED LISTENING SKILLS CAN BOOST SALES SUCCESS

Date:
5/17/04

Meeting:
Northeast Regional Sales Staff

Circle the number that best rates the speaker in the following categories. If the speaker deserves a top score, circle number one.

1. Presented useful information:

    1, 2, 3, 4, 5

2. Backed up assertions with facts:

    1, 2, 3, 4, 5

3. Easy to listen to and understand:

    1, 2, 3, 4, 5

4. Visual aids enhanced the program:

    1, 2, 3, 4, 5

5. I'd give the speaker an overall rating of:

    1, 2, 3, 4, 5

Here's something else I noticed: _____

_____

_____

If you're generating a one-page evaluation and you'd rather not let ratings be anonymous, simply repeat the questions in the slot designated for a specific person. For example:

BETTY BONNET

1. _____

2. _____

3. _____

4. _____

5. _____

Other comments: _____

_____

_____

TRENT PICKE

1. _____

2. _____

3. _____

4. _____

5. _____

Other comments: _____

_____

_____

◆

This evaluation isn't a scientific study, so don't concern yourself with the purity factor. If one person is influenced by seeing another person's rating choices, so be it.

ADDED VALUE

When a person takes a moment to evaluate the speaker, he automatically takes a moment to reflect on what transpired. This review can be the stimulus that moves a person from thinking about a new idea to getting ready to act on it.

Practical tips and techniques that help meeting attendees achieve goals are what the best speakers leave behind. As a result, your call for an evaluation may help to achieve more than meets the eye.

Chapter 12

Wrapping It Up:

When Is Enough Enough?

"I shall sit here," the Footman remarked, *"till tomorrow—or the next day, maybe."*

—Alice's Adventures in Wonderland

"It ain't over till it's over." Truer words were never spoken when it comes to meetings. There are two kinds of meeting time: agenda time—the hours and minutes *scheduled* for the meeting—and real time—how long the meeting actually takes. If you do your job as meeting leader properly, *real time should never be longer than agenda time.* And it never hurts if it's a bit shorter.

When should you end a meeting? The answer is, when the work has been accomplished or the allotted time for the meeting is up, whichever comes first. You should never carry a meeting past its announced conclusion time, because other participants have tight schedules and commitments in other places. They have met their half of the bargain by agreeing to your announced time frame; it's your responsibility to meet your half by sticking to it. If there's a crisis—a situation in which work has to be completed immediately regardless of how long it takes—all participants should be notified of this *in advance* of the meeting so that they can be prepared to stay indefinitely.

It is advisable to end a meeting before its scheduled conclusion if your purpose has been accomplished *or* if the proceedings are hopelessly bogged down. If your discussion seems to be going in circles and nothing you do to try to get it back on track is working, then it's time to stop for the day and reschedule.

Like a good book, a well-run meeting has a structure. There is a beginning, a middle, and an end. Why is the end of the meeting important? Why not wait for the bell to ring, slam the book shut in midsentence, and walk out?

The first reason is courtesy: The participants, who have committed their time and energy to work with you, deserve better than rudeness. There are certain formalities that are expected and appreciated in the course of human interaction, one of which is finishing properly what you've started.

The end of a meeting is more than a formality, however. It includes important business and sets the stage for the next phase of action.

There really is no *one* end to a meeting. Rather, there is a series of endings that culminates in the final wrap-up. As discussed in previous chapters, the meeting process involves several stages: Information is presented; then it is discussed; decisions are made; and, finally, actions are agreed on. Each of these stages must be ended properly before moving on to the next. Further, depending on the content of the meeting, each stage may include substages that must also be finished before the meeting moves on. For example, if the meeting involves the presentation and discussion of several topics, each one must be introduced and analyzed in an orderly fashion. For the meeting leader, this requires the skillful opening and closing of many discussions. These "mini-endings," as we will see, are simply minor variations on the process of ending the meeting.

If the meeting has been ticking along on time, you can wrap it up more easily than if the hour grows late. Here are some strategies that enable you to attain that goal:

DESIGNATE AN OFFICIAL TIMEKEEPER

If all assembled know at the onset that speakers have a limited time to address the group, the designation of a timekeeper will be viewed as matter-of-fact.

USE VISUAL SIGNALS

A small yellow flag can be raised when four minutes pass. A red flag signals that time is up. The timekeeper raises the flags, as needed. It's a polite way to keep speakers mindful of time restraints. This technique silently announces an equal time policy, too. Accordingly, each person's sense of fairness should contribute to her willingness to cooperate.

CENSORSHIP

You might be tempted to censor a speaker if you're not in agreement with what's being discussed, but you're well advised to be more indulgent. Don't censor someone who follows the rules of the meeting. If the subject appears on the agenda and the individual is within time limits when he speaks, don't bang the gavel and signal time to stop.

The most predictable spot for an aggrieved individual to seek remedy is when the meeting is about to end. You're probably more vulnerable because you're in a relaxed mode, believing your hard work is finished. A person you censor can throw a monkey wrench into the finale if he persists. If you pull rank, you invite sympathy for the purportedly injured party. You sidestep this scenario when you refuse to silence bona fide speakers. (Note: If you're censored and seeking remedy, consider pleading your case near the end of the proceedings.)

In the dictionary, the word *conclusion* has several related meanings: the end of something, the outcome or result of a process, a judgment or decision reached after deliberation, a final settlement, and the closing of a discourse that contains a summing up. This, then, is what you are doing when you end a meeting: The meeting is concluded.

Concluding a meeting is a three-step process: preparing the group for the conclusion, wrapping up the findings and decisions, and expressing appreciation for the work accomplished.

1. **Preparing to Conclude the Meeting.** The meeting leader is in many ways like a director of a play: He or she is the only participant who has an overall view, a perspective on the entire stage. The other players have their individual interests and preoccupations; the leader watches out for the group. For this reason, it is necessary to prepare the meeting participants for the end of the session.

You can do this simply by saying, ten minutes before the meeting is over, "Let's wrap it up, folks; we have to be out of here in a few minutes." This gives the participants time to organize their thoughts, have a last word, and mentally sum up for themselves what the meeting has meant. It starts them thinking about the next step—what actions they need to take from this point on.

2. **Wrapping It Up.** Wrapping up a meeting means summarizing the proceedings for the group, including repeating the meeting's purpose, and then outlining what happened. You'll be telling people what they just heard, and because this may cause some listeners to tune out, you'll want to adapt a pattern for evaluating the meeting that keeps people's attention riveted to your review. Accentuate the positive. Deliver your comments with energy and power. These are important and timely tips because you may feel drained when the meeting is drawing to a close. If necessary, attach small sticky notes to the last page of your notes so you don't forget this advice.

"Nothing great was ever achieved without enthusiasm." You may want to adapt these seven words, written by Ralph Waldo Emerson, as your personal guideline.

Be sure to summarize what was discussed, what decisions were made, and what, if anything, was *not* accomplished. You should also emphasize what actions will be taken on the basis of the decisions made, who will take those actions, and when the work is expected to be completed.

Here's an illustration: BMW's new division, Mini USA, brought back a "lovable English motoring mite," the Mini Cooper. (John Gaffney wrote about the award-winning marketing campaign in the May 2002 issue of *www.business2.com*). The reintroduction plan showcased the cars, which are nothing like conventional BMWs. The Mini measures 11 feet, 10 inches from bumper to bumper, making it the shortest car on the road.

If you were a fly on the wall at marketing strategy meetings, you might have heard participants discuss how potential buyers were likely to be risk takers, nonconformists. Accordingly, advertising for the Mini Cooper would not be conventional. Instead of early television and magazine exposure, the car made its appearance on top of another car! Among other things, this meant assuring BMW's legal department that the ploy wouldn't represent a safety breach. When magazine ads finally ran, they ran along the margins of editorial pages, boasting, "Nothing corners like a Mini." The planners didn't stop here. When it was all said and done, they sold Minis and brought home a coveted advertising industry award—Sweet Spot Awards, Most Innovative Campaign.

These marketers probably met often and were masterful summarizers. How else could they have kept this exciting campaign on track? They likely asked themselves questions such as, What did we discuss? What are we doing about it? Who has a need to know? Who will take responsibility? What didn't we accomplish? Is that okay? What next?

3. Expressing Appreciation. In concluding the meeting, be sure to thank the participants. This should include a collective thank-you to the group and recognition of individual contributions that were significant to the success of the meeting. Many meeting leaders make the mistake of limiting their words of appreciation to "Thanks for coming today." The fact is that most of those in attendance probably had no choice in the matter; they were there because they were compelled in one way or another. A more appropriate expression of appreciation might be, "Thank you for your contributions and the time you've taken to think about what we've discussed. Your help has been appreciated."

Chapter 13

Thumbs Up or Down:

Assessing the Meeting

"If there's no meaning in it," said the King,
"that saves a world of trouble, you know,
as we needn't try to find any."

—*Alice's Adventures in Wonderland*

Most of us go through life placing values on our impressions and experiences: "What a beauty!" "That was a great meal!" "I loved that movie!" We evaluate, according to our standards and tastes, what we see, feel, hear, or taste. Why? Why not just say, "That was a meal," or "That was a movie," or "That was a meeting"? There are several reasons.

An evaluation makes something complete. It helps us to shape and give meaning to an experience, and this, in turn, allows us to place the experience in perspective. The human animal needs to create an order in which to live; chaos doesn't work. To evaluate something is to give order to it and to our relationship to it.

Assessing or evaluating a meeting allows us to say, "Yes, I understand what this means. I know what importance it has. I know what to do with it. I know the next step to take." Without such an assessment, a meeting is an experience without value to its participants. Without an assessment there is no way to determine whether the meeting's purpose was achieved, thus making the meeting purposeless.

In the simplest terms the meeting assessment answers three questions:

◆ What happened?

◆ What was accomplished?

◆ What was not accomplished?

By answering those questions, you are able to organize your thoughts, understand the significance of the decisions made at the meeting, plan the next step, and identify areas of possible improvement in your skills.

The core of an assessment is the summary of the proceedings you make at the conclusion of the meeting. This summary outlines the facts and ideas introduced and the decisions made at the meeting. The next step is to place a value on these and other actions—to rate the meeting. The most efficient way to assess a meeting is to use a checklist for your personal reference. Remember that although elements of your assessment will be incorporated into a final, public report on the meeting, the checklist is essentially for your confidential use. It is a tool for self-improvement.

The checklist that follows is intended only as a guide; you may require fewer or more entries, depending on the specifics of your meeting. Most, but not all, questions can be answered *yes* or *no*. In determining how you might have handled the meeting differently, be sure to be specific and comprehensive.

MEETING ASSESSMENT CHECKLIST

Meeting Purpose or Objective
Was it designed to generate concrete results (decisions, actions)?
Was the accomplishment of the purpose measurable?
Was the purpose or objective achievable (realistic)?
How could I have structured the objective differently?

Participants
Were the right number of people invited?
Was the selection of the participants successful?
How could I have improved the participant list?

Preparations
Were invitations extended on time?
Were invitations followed up?
Was my preparation of materials adequate?
Were participants prepared to discuss the topics of the meeting?

Were facilities and equipment arranged in time?
Were supplies adequate?
How could I have prepared for the meeting differently?

Quality of Discussion

Was there adequate discussion of topics?
Was group participation adequate?
Were all topics discussed?
Was enough time allotted for discussion?
How could I have managed the discussion phase of the meeting differently?

Decision Making

Were decisions made at the meeting?
Did the decisions help accomplish the purpose of the meeting?
Was there enough time to make all the decisions required?
Was the information provided in the meeting adequate for making decisions?
How could I have handled the decision-making phase of the meeting differently?

Assignments

Were assignments for future action made on the basis of the decisions?
Did the assignments help accomplish the purpose of the meeting?
Did all participants leave the meeting with a clear understanding of their next task?
Is there a system in place to ensure that appropriate follow-ups will be made on actions to be taken?
How could I have made assignments differently?

Collaterals

Did collateral materials reinforce the subject(s) of the meeting?
Were the collaterals easily digested without being distracting to participants?
Were collaterals distributed at the right time?
How could the collaterals have been different?

Audiovisuals

Did the audiovisuals enhance the presentation?
Did they appropriately reflect the image of the company or speaker?
Should there have been more (or fewer) visuals?
Could audiovisuals have been used differently?

Timing

Did the meeting start on time?
Were all participants on time?
Did the meeting end on time?
Was there adequate time for the meeting?
How could I have structured the time element of the meeting differently?

Handling Problems

What problems were encountered during the meeting?
Were the problems adequately resolved?
How could I have handled the problems differently?

Chapter 14

Writing It Up:

Reporting the Results

"Take pen and ink, and write it down."

—*Alice's Adventures in Wonderland*

If the opera isn't over until the fat lady sings, a meeting isn't over until you've written it up. By the end of a few strenuous hours in a conference room, the last thing you may want to do is give the meeting more thought, but a clearly written report of the proceedings will be an invaluable tool for several reasons. You should be sure to make this effort.

THE PURPOSE OF THE FINAL REPORT

The final report on a meeting is a synopsis of the proceedings, including whatever decisions and actions were agreed on. Depending on the nature of the meeting, other follow-up materials may have to be prepared, such as research papers, surveys, market studies, proposals, and presentations, but the one document that must be completed for every meeting is the final report.

The final report accomplishes several things:

1. **It Provides a Written Record of the Meeting's Proceedings.** The human memory is an often unreliable tool; a document that describes the proceedings, although it certainly does not present a total, completely objective picture, at least provides a source to which people can refer for information, a record that, once written, does not change. People record meetings to preserve a verbatim account of proceedings. (Be aware that some participants will stifle comments when they're being recorded.) If you choose to record meetings, use a tape recorder, camcorder, or modern-day tools to get the job done. Real-time sound recorder software such as Audio Record Wizard 3 and digital dictation products such as Olympus DS-2000 Digital Voice are easy to locate on the Internet. New and efficient recording devices show up from time to time. Use them as needed.

2. **The Final Report Makes Follow-Up Easier.** A well-run meeting concludes with the assignment of further actions. A written report helps you and others remember to carry out those tasks and reinforces a sense of responsibility for those assignments. The report also serves to clarify the assignments, distinguishing between long-term and short-term projects, and provides participants a timetable to work with.

3. **The Report Reminds All Participants of the Content of the Meeting, Any Decisions Made and Their Significance to Each Individual's Work.** By reinforcing the ideas discussed during the meeting, the report keeps those ideas alive and stimulates their further consideration.

In summary, the final report puts into writing everything you concluded in the meeting and provides a vision of what happened and what must happen in the future. Because it is in writing and readily accessible, it acts as a reinforcement to your goals and helps you accomplish them.

4. **It Praises People for a Job Well Done.** The final report should acknowledge the work of all those involved and, in particular, anyone whose efforts were extraordinary.

ILLUSTRATION: The warehouse manager attended the 10 A.M. meeting at corporate headquarters just after working the night shift at the warehouse. Normally, he would have gone home to sleep. The warehouse is some forty-five minutes drive time from corporate offices and in the opposite direction of his home.

Your final report of the meeting says, "Mr. John Hawkes, Driscoll Hall warehouse manager, attended the March 30th meeting on his own time. His input regarding real-time requirements for merchandise turnaround eliminated the need for guesswork. John's assessment and valuable support permitted the committee to move forward without reservation. Thank you, John!"

ILLUSTRATION: A computer glitch made it necessary for one secretary to update figures from handwritten logs. It was tedious, painstaking work. The meeting report says, "The committee owes Mary Gladstone sincere thanks. Mary's ingenuity and industry made it possible for the committee to have up-to-the-minute figures available in spite of the computer shutdown."

THE FORM OF THE FINAL REPORT

Choose your report vocabulary with care. Avoid cliches. Say what you mean. Not only should you take the time to condense your report, but you'll want to choose your words with care. On occasion, however, it may be useful to repeat an idea using different words. It's a good ploy to use when a concept isn't easy to explain. A doctor at a psychiatric clinic told his listeners that some patients may have a mental illness and then get well. He added, "And then they may even get weller." He went on to explain he meant they get better than they were before.

This illustration also underscores how creative use of vocabulary can serve a useful purpose. In general, short and sweet is a good rule of thumb. An upbeat writing style that accentuates the positive creates a report that's most likely to be read and remembered.

Take care not to be judgmental, tempting though it may be. The meeting report should contain little more than the facts. Judging whom to praise and how to express that praise is one acceptable exception to this rule.

Unless you have specific instructions to the contrary, the final report should be an elaboration of the minutes of the meeting. Properly recorded, the minutes should outline the entire proceedings of the meeting. They should include the ideas discussed (with contributions identified by participant) and decisions and assignments made, recording the proceedings in the order in which they took place.

The final report consists of the minutes (usually prepared by someone other than the meeting leader) plus your comments, observations, and corrections. The report should be as short as possible, in expanded outline form. You should avoid large blocks of dense copy; use short, declarative statements that express your thoughts in as few words as possible. Remember, you want the report to be read, not discarded; make it look appealing and quickly digestible.

Depending on the meeting, there may be more than one final report. As you conclude the meeting, you may need to ask for reports from other participants on specific aspects of the discussion. These documents should be included with or assimilated into your final report.

DISTRIBUTION OF THE FINAL REPORT

The distribution of the final report depends on the corporate structure of your company. Certainly your boss should get a copy, as should every participant. If the decisions made at the meeting might be of interest or help to other departments, the report should be sent to appropriate personnel in those departments. The report should be kept on file in case anyone else needs to see it.

The final report should be prepared and delivered as quickly as possible. If it is simply an expanded version of the minutes, it should be completed within three or four days. If there are other documents that will take time to prepare, send out the edited minutes of the meeting immediately with a note saying that the final report, with other papers, will follow shortly.

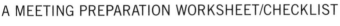

A MEETING PREPARATION WORKSHEET/CHECKLIST

<u>Purpose of Meeting</u> (in 25 words or less):

<u>Place</u>:

<u>Date</u>:

<u>Time</u>:

<u>List of Participants</u>   <u>Date Invited</u>   <u>Date Confirmed</u>

<u>Materials for Meeting</u>   <u>Date Completed</u>

<u>To Do on Day of Meeting</u>   <u>Done</u>

Check location
Check supplies and materials
Check catering
Telephone reminder to participants

Follow-Up to Meeting	Date Due	Date Completed
Minutes of the meeting		
Follow-up telephone calls		
Follow-up reports (list)		
Final report/analysis		

Note: Depending on your position, the responsibility for ensuring that all the necessary preparations for the meeting are carried out may be yours or your assistant's. In either case, using a checklist is a good idea.

INDEX

More selected BARRON'S titles: